NATIONAL AUDUBON SOCIETY

Birder's Handbook

NATIONAL AUDUBON SOCIETY

Birder's Handbook

Stephen W. Kress

DORLING KINDERSLEY

LONDON, NEW YORK, DELHI, JOHANNESBURG, MUNICH, PARIS, and SYDNEY

www.dk.com

In memory of Irving Kassoy, who shared his enthusiasm for watching birds.

A DORLING KINDERSLEY BOOK

Produced by The Moschovitis Group, Inc.
www.mosgroup.com

Senior Editor: Hilary W. Poole
Art Director and Designer: Annemarie Redmond
Photo Research: Gillian Speeth
Illustrations: Grant Jerding, Anne Senechal Faust
Editorial Coordinator: Stephanie Schreiber
Editorial Assistant: Renée Miller
Copyediting and Proofreading: Brady Kahn and Anita Seaberg
Production Assistant: Yolanda Pluguez
Index: AEIOU, Inc.

First American Edition, 2000
2 4 6 8 10 9 7 5 3 1

Published in the United States by
Dorling Kindersley Publishing, Inc.
95 Madison Avenue
New York, New York 10016

Library of Congress Cataloging-in-Publication Data
Kress, Stephen W.
    National Audubon Society birder's handbook / Stephen W. Kress.—1st
American ed.
        p. cm.
    ISBN 0-7894-5153-0 (alk. paper)
    1. Bird watching. I. Title: Birder's Handbook. II. National Audubon
Society. III. Title.
QL67.5.K74 2000
598'.07'234—dc21   99-050061
                                                        CIP

Reproduced by Progressive Information Technologies, United States
Printed and bound in China by L.Rex Printing Company Limited

CONTENTS

PREFACE

Every ornithologist and birder can recall the moment that ignited her or his passion for birds. Often that moment comes at a very early age, in the company of a mentor. I recall my epiphany one day in June 1950 when my beloved grandfather, Frank Rockingham Downing, pointed to a little brown bird in the bird-bath, offered me his old binoculars (which smelled wonderfully of leather, sweat, and oil), and said, "That's a Song Sparrow. It has a large spot on its breast." In just two minutes, my world changed. I discovered the power of binoculars, the power of knowing the name of a wild creature, and, most of all, the power of birds.

Once you start, it's hard to stop. There are always new birds to see and new things to learn. A passion for birds can lead to learning about their voices, behavior, ecology, and distribution. Naming birds leads to a compulsion to count them. Better than telling a friend that "I saw a Red-headed Woodpecker" is saying, "I saw two Red-headed Woodpeckers." Best of all is the satisfaction of sharing discoveries with others.

The potential value of birds as a scientific and an educational tool for citizens of all ages and occupations has never been greater. Skills in naming and counting birds quickly qualify bird-watchers to contribute to our knowledge. Thousands of people of all ages and backgrounds participate in professional research projects dealing with birds. From backyards to remote forests, these "citizen scientists" represent the world's largest organized research team.

The Internet now offers an unprecedented opportunity for people to share bird discoveries. In particular, BirdSource available at http://birdsource.org, an initiative of the National Audubon Society and Cornell Laboratory of Ornithology, provides a forum for bird-literate oldsters to help computer-literate youngsters

discover and value nature through birds. One project, the Great Backyard Bird Count, engages citizens throughout the continent. In February of this year, participants from throughout the United States and Canada joined forces in a global project. They recorded bird sightings from backyards, neighborhoods, or city parks—over 42,000 checklists and over 3 million birds. They watched their data appear instantaneously on maps that displayed, with staggering accuracy and detail, the abundance and distributions of 342 bird species across North America. Best of all, the participants discovered the power of birds, which one birdwatcher encapsulated with these words: "I had the most wonderful surprise as I watched the backyard I thought I knew. The crowning glory was a drift of Cedar Waxwings—never before seen here—for a twenty-second landing on a pine tree, as we watched! It was entertaining and educational at the same time, and frankly, breathtaking."

I joined the senior staff of the National Audubon Society three years ago for one reason—to connect people to nature through birds. Prominent among my new colleagues on the staff was Steve Kress. A pioneer in the restoration of seabird colonies, especially our beloved Atlantic Puffins, Steve also has been a leader in connecting people to nature through birds. In this second edition of the *National Audubon Society Birders Handbook*, Steve reaches out to the growing community of people with a passion for birds—helping novice and serious birders alike increase their skills. Knowledgeable birders will become the most effective stewards of our wild birds.

Frank Gill
National Audubon Society
June 1999

INTRODUCTION

The first edition of the *National Audubon Society Birder's Handbook* was published in 1981 when bird watching was already recognized as one of the fastest growing outdoor activities in North America. Its popularity has continued to grow. A 1996 U.S. Fish and Wildlife Service study tallied more than 42 million backyard bird-watchers in the United States. The study found that one out of five adults in the U.S. watches or feeds birds, and that bird enthusiasts collectively spend over $8.2 billion on equipment and supplies such as binoculars, film, and bird food! To put this number in perspective, more people watch birds than pursue consumptive wildlife sports such as freshwater angling and hunting (30 and 14 million, respectively). This interest presents an enormous opportunity to further the cause of bird conservation.

The purpose of this book remains the same as the first edition: to provide an introductory techniques manual and source book for bird-watchers to help them become more capable "citizen scientists." Many ongoing research and monitoring programs depend on amateur birders for collecting massive amounts of data, a requirement for conducting continent-wide assessments of bird populations. No other branch of science is as well-endowed with enthusiastic amateurs as ornithology.

A recent study by the U.S. Fish and Wildlife Service reports that committed bird-watchers outshine other animal-oriented groups—such as zoo enthusiasts, pet owners, trappers, and supporters of animal welfare causes—by consistently demonstrating a "sophisticated and well-balanced environmental protection attitude." The study also found that serious bird-watchers were the best-informed group on a broad range of ecological and animal-life topics.

This research supports a widely held belief within the bird watching community—that an interest in birds is often a first step toward building a sound conservation ethic. Because birds are sensitive indicators of the health of our environment, it is likely that a popular commitment to their well-being will lead to a more widespread concern for the quality of the environment on which we and the birds are mutually dependent. The conspicuous and appealing nature of birds makes them ideal candidates to carry the message that we and the birds depend on intact ecosystems where humans and wildlife can flourish. The presence of diverse bird populations, capable of sustained reproduction, is one of the best indicators of a healthy environment.

Approximately ten thousand species of birds occur in the world and about eight hundred of these occur in North America. Keen observers in North America can find more than one hundred species in or flying over most suburban backyards. For this reason, the best place to begin watching birds is at home. Start by identifying the birds that frequent your yard or nearby park and do everything possible to improve your own property or local wildlife habitats. Take pride in the number of species you can encourage to nest or feed, but beware that bird identification and list keeping should not become ends in themselves. To enjoy birds fully, keep observing after you've made identifications. The same excitement that comes from discovering "new" birds can be found by pursuing new activities and learning more about familiar birds.

This book is intended for both the beginning and experienced amateur bird-watcher. The beginner will find basic instructions on how to identify birds and select binoculars and photography equipment, while both the beginner and the experienced birder will benefit from discussions of such fun field activities as sketching, note taking, counting, photography, and sound recording.

Since publication of the first edition of this book in 1981, the number of opportunities for amateurs to assist bird conservation projects has exploded. Then, a national search found fewer than two hundred programs, a

number that has more than doubled in the intervening twenty years. Likewise, there is an explosion of choices for taking national and international bird tours—far too many to include here. For these birding adventures, it's best to consult local bird clubs and Audubon chapters and to scan the advertisements in bird-watching magazines.

I could not have written this book without the enthusiastic support and encouragement of many people. I thank Robert M. Beck, Greg Budney, William C. Dilger, Tim Gallagher, Daniel Gray, Steven G. Herman, Michael J. Hopiak, Donald A. McCrimmon, Jr., Kevin McGowan, Ken Rosenberg, and Alvan E. Staffan for reading sections of the manuscript and offering suggestions for its improvement. I also appreciate the assistance received in assembling materials from Diane DeLuca, Marie

Eckhardt, Thomas L. Fleischner, Ann James, Terry Mingle, Sandy Podulka, and Ron Rohrbaugh.

It is my pleasure to acknowledge the imaginative art of my illustrators, Anne Senechal Faust and Grant Jerding. It is also a pleasure to acknowledge the editorial guidance received from Hilary W. Poole and Stephanie Schreiber, whose great efforts brought this new edition to life. I also thank Beth Campbell for her very capable assistance typing both editions of this book.

Throughout my preparation of the manuscript, I found ready support for my principal purpose in writing the book—to provide a guide that would demonstrate that bird-watching can be a lifelong pursuit that becomes more enjoyable as the years go by. I hope the book accomplishes its purpose, for I believe it will be a happier and gentler world as more people take the time to watch the birds.

Stephen W. Kress
September 1999

CHAPTER ONE

BIRDING TECHNIQUES

You'll find birds wherever you go, but the best place to begin watching them is at home, where repeated observation will sharpen your birding skills. Start by looking for the features of shape, size, posture, and behavior that permit you to place a bird in the correct family. Once you have determined the family, the number of possibilities is greatly reduced, and you only need to consider those members of the family that are likely to be in this specific habitat at this time of year. Listen for song and look for field marks to make your final decision as to which species you are watching.

IDENTIFYING BIRDS

The ability to identify birds is largely a matter of familiarity. It is much like getting to know human neighbors. Move into a new community, and at first everyone is a stranger, but soon neighbors are easy to recognize on the street, and a mere word over the telephone can identify the caller. The ability to distinguish personalities, faces, and voices is mainly a matter of repeated contact and attention to detail. Look for the characteristics of the birds that visit your yard and you'll start to notice similarities and differences among them. Here are some things to consider when identifying a bird.

Shape

Professional ornithologists group birds into families that contain closely related species. If you learn to recognize birds by family characteristics—such as the shape of body, wings, tail, and beak—it soon becomes easy to place unknown birds in the correct families and then proceed to look for specific field marks such as color patterns. Knowledge of families is also invaluable when you are traveling, because it becomes easy to place unknown species in already familiar families and then proceed to the correct identification by relying on other clues such as field marks, size, behavior, and location.

THE FAT AND THE SKINNY

Take a close look at birds and you'll soon note many different shapes. Birds of approximately the same size vary dramatically in body shape and proportion. Some, like doves and pigeons, have chunky bodies, while others, such as cuckoos, have slender ones. Knowledge of bird shapes will even permit you to recognize birds by their characteristic silhouettes.

Black-billed Cuckoo

The cuckoo's long tail accentuates its slender body.

Band-tailed Pigeon

Crows are among our largest perching birds.

American Crow

Size

After shape, size is the next most important consideration. Size is most useful for making comparisons. Comparisons are helpful if you see an unknown bird in close proximity to a familiar bird whose size you know, but with some practice you can rely on your memory for reference—a raspberry-colored bird the size of a House Sparrow may be a Purple Finch. Without a careful size comparison, it could be confused with a Pine Grosbeak, which has similar colors and patterns but is almost as big as a robin.

Be cautious when considering size—especially at a distance when there are no other birds nearby for comparison. Apparent size can be distorted by lighting conditions and distance, and can be especially confusing at dusk and dawn and under conditions of fog and rain. Although birds of the same species are usually similar in size, you can sometimes note a size difference between males and females. For example, male gulls, geese, and pheasants are larger than females of the same species, but female hawks, eagles, and owls are larger than males.

American Robin

House Sparrow

COMMON COMPARISIONS
The American Crow, American Robin, and House Sparrow are common birds throughout most of North America and can serve as size references for comparison with less familiar birds.

Some hummingbirds have been clocked at a wingbeat of as many as 80 strokes per second while in forward flight.

Broad-billed Hummingbird

Northern Cardinal

THE EFFECTS OF WEATHER
Birds can change their apparent size depending on the weather. When the temperature is hot, birds can sleek their feathers tight to their bodies, which makes them look smaller. On frigid winter days they may fluff themselves up, providing better insulation and a much larger appearance.

Birds often make such quick appearances that they do not give the observer a chance to methodically go through the steps of identification. With practice and repetition, most birders find that they use these tips almost at once, and they are even able to process a "blur of a bird" by shape, size, behavior, time of year, and other clues.

Posture

You can usually place birds in the proper family by looking for similarities in posture. Watch a robin strut across the yard—it takes several steps forward, followed by an alert, upright stance. Other members of the thrush family have similar posture.

Eastern Wood-Pewee

In contrast, the Cape May Warbler perches in a horizontal posture.

Flycatchers typically perch with a very erect stance.

Flight Pattern

Birds also have characteristic flight patterns. Note that finches have a steep, roller-coaster flight pattern, while woodpeckers usually fly in a deep, undulating manner. Even the way a bird holds its wings while in flight may be useful in making an identification. Turkey Vultures, for example, are easily distinguished from Black Vultures, hawks, and eagles by the position of their wings as they soar.

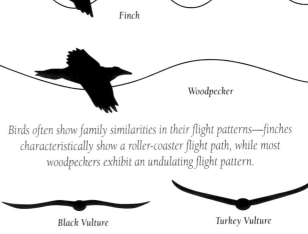

Finch

Woodpecker

Birds often show family similarities in their flight patterns—finches characteristically show a roller-coaster flight path, while most woodpeckers exhibit an undulating flight pattern.

Black Vulture

Turkey Vulture

Turkey Vultures hold their wings at an upward angle over their backs, while Black Vultures, hawks, and eagles hold their wings on a level plane.

Behavior

Birds often have unique behaviors that distinguish them from closely related species in the same family. Such behaviors help birds recognize other members of their own species. The same behaviors can also help you make bird identifications. If you spot a slim bird sitting with an upright posture on a dead branch, it will likely be a member of the flycatcher family. If you observe it fly out, snatch an insect out of midair, and then return to the same perch, it probably is a flycatcher, since few other birds exhibit this "hawking" behavior. If the bird starts wagging its tail, you can be certain that it is a phoebe—a medium-sized flycatcher that characteristically flicks its tail up and down. Since there are various kinds of phoebes, you would then have to refer to a field guide to find the differences in range and specific field marks.

Cape May Warbler

Say's Phoebe

After you have placed a bird in its proper family, watch it carefully for characteristic behaviors. For example, phoebes are the only flycatchers to engage in tail-wagging behaviors.

Warblers and vireos look very similar. Both families contain small, insect-eating birds that live high in trees. If you have the opportunity to observe them feeding, it will soon become apparent that warblers are quick, energetic feeders that seldom stay in one place as they pick tiny insects from leaves and branches. In contrast vireos often perch in one place, waiting until they see a large insect—then they dash forward to snatch their prey.

Blue-headed Vireo

Field Marks

The same distinctive patterns and colors that make birds so appealing to humans often serve as species identification signals for other birds. The bold markings on male ducks, for example, usually ensure that the females have no difficulty in finding a male of their own species. Conspicuous color patterns reduce the chance of interbreeding and the production of hybrids, which are often infertile or poorly adapted.

Field marks are also a useful aid to bird-watchers. Even inconspicuous markings may be useful to both birds and birders when it comes to distinguishing similar-looking species. Look the bird over for such markings as wing bars, eye rings, eye lines, eye stripes, crests, wing patches, and tail spots.

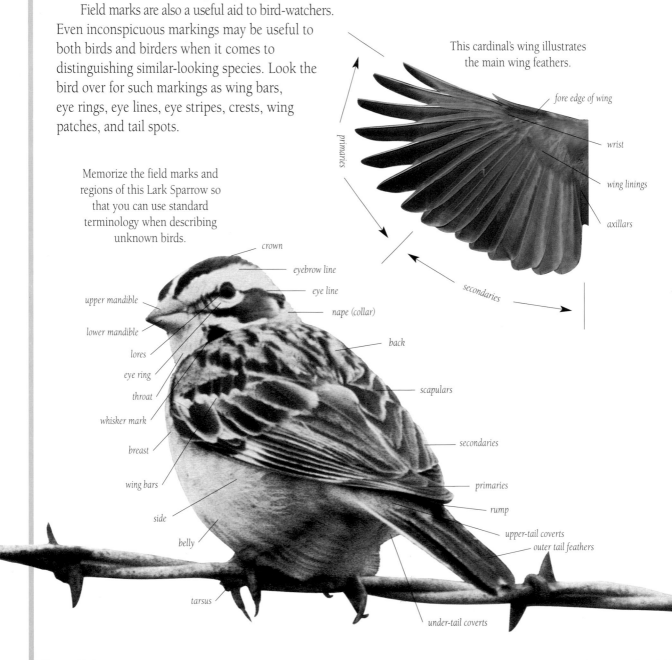

This cardinal's wing illustrates the main wing feathers.

fore edge of wing

wrist

wing linings

axillars

primaries

secondaries

Memorize the field marks and regions of this Lark Sparrow so that you can use standard terminology when describing unknown birds.

crown

eyebrow line

eye line

nape (collar)

upper mandible

lower mandible

lores

eye ring

throat

whisker mark

breast

wing bars

side

belly

tarsus

back

scapulars

secondaries

primaries

rump

upper-tail coverts

outer tail feathers

under-tail coverts

Color

Although color can sometimes be a useful aid in bird identification, it is usually much better to rely on such clues as shape, posture, and behavior, since the apparent color of a bird often varies with the angle of view and the lighting situation. Birds such as tanagers, warblers, and shorebirds experience complete body molts, during which all of their bright breeding-color feathers are lost as they change into more somber winter plumage. Meanwhile, individual birds often vary in the amount of color they display, depending on age, sex, and the time of year. Also remember that it is confusing to make exact comparisons of living birds with color plates in field guides, since color reproductions only approximate bird colors and the quality of the color varies from one printing to the next.

Patterns of contrasting color are more useful than actual colors. Patterns such as striped breasts, dark caps, and light-colored rumps are visible under most lighting conditions. For example, the markings of the Golden-crowned Kinglet should be conspicuous even at a considerable distance.

Many birds perch upright in an exposed location when singing on territory.

Song

The primary function of bird song is to announce the presence of the singer by broadcasting the territorial message. Male songbirds defend their territories primarily through singing displays. The songs and calls of birds are useful to bird-watchers because they often announce the identity of birds that would be otherwise overlooked in dense vegetation. Familiarity with bird songs usually comes after learning to recognize birds by their appearance. Recordings of bird songs do not take the place of field experience, but they are useful for review of songs heard outdoors. Like identifying birds by sight, song recognition comes only after much practice in the field. The best way to learn bird song is to concentrate on one song at a time and pursue the unknown singer until you get a good enough view to establish its identity.

Eastern Meadowlark

Habitat

Birds are predictably associated with specific habitats. Bitterns, for example, are usually found in cattail marshes and usually live in association with other freshwater marsh birds: you are less likely to find a bittern in a salt-marsh habitat. Each plant community, such as a spruce-fir forest, a meadow, or a freshwater marsh, has a predictable assemblage of birds, which is part of the community. Learn which birds to expect in each habitat, and you'll be able to eliminate many similar species that are usually associated with other habitats.

IDENTIFYING SIMILAR-LOOKING BIRDS
Knowledge of habitat is one of the best ways to identify similar-looking birds such as the Alder, Least, and Acadian flycatchers pictured here. These small flycatchers all have white eye rings and wing bars. They are so similar in appearance that they are not easily told apart—even if they were held in the hand. The birds probably recognize members of their own species by their distinctive songs and preferences for different habitats.

Alder Flycatchers live in wet, marshy habitats.

Least Flycatchers live in upland forest borders.

Acadian Flycatchers live in moist woodlands.

CAMOUFLAGE
Bitterns are easily camouflaged in their usual marshland habitat and seldom visit other habitats. But because birds often migrate over a variety of habitats between their breeding and wintering homes, they sometimes show up in surprising places. During spring and fall migrations, birds often settle down when they become tired, regardless of where they are. Tired bitterns like the one pictured here sometimes land in grassy backyards, but being so accustomed to hiding among cattails, they still hold their heads in a characteristic vertical posture.

Range and Abundance

Although birds are highly mobile and often show up in out-of-the-way places, they are usually very predictable about staying within defined geographic limits, known as ranges. General information about bird distribution is readily available in any of the field guides. Those with maps are the easiest to use in the field.

Just as it is important to know which species you might see, it is also helpful to know something of the relative abundance of different species. Learn the common birds first—then you will be more likely to spot birds that look different. Remember, however, that birds don't pay attention to range maps or read books. Ranges change and wandering individuals occur in most species. Your alert observations can help to document such events.

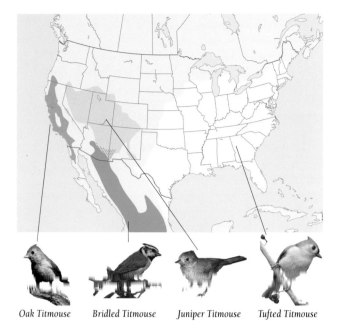

Oak Titmouse   *Bridled Titmouse*   *Juniper Titmouse*   *Tufted Titmouse*

TITMOUSE RANGE MAP

Range maps are one of the most important tools in establishing which of several common species you are most likely to see. For example, the ranges shown on this map for four species of titmouse do not usually overlap and are useful in showing which species one might expect to see.

Time of Year

It is useful to know which birds visit your locale at different times of the year. By knowing which birds to expect at each season, you can sometimes tell similar-looking species apart. Some closely related species neatly divide the year with little overlap.

TREE SPARROW OR FIELD SPARROW?

The ranges of the American Tree Sparrow and Field Sparrow overlap, but the Tree Sparrow occurs in winter, while the Field Sparrow occurs after the Tree Sparrow has headed back north. Tree Sparrows breed in the northern tundra and invade northern states only during the winter. About the time the last of the Tree Sparrows head north, the Field Sparrows arrive from their winter habitat in the southern United States. Both species are seldom seen at the same time. Specific field marks, such as the Tree Sparrow's black chest spot and the Field Sparrow's pink bill, will confirm the identification.

Field Sparrow

American Tree Sparrow

CLOSING THE DISTANCE

The greatest problem for beginning bird-watchers is the distance that most birds prefer to keep between themselves and observers. Since most birds are usually wary of close approaches and quickly take flight or retreat into dense vegetation, it is useful to have a few tricks to help close the distance between you and the birds.

Red-winged Blackbird

Pishing

To attract land birds, try imitating the generalized distress call, known as pishing, that many birds give when they are alarmed. This call sounds like the word "pish" pronounced as a drawn-out, hissing exhale. It is most effective during nesting season, when birds are protecting their territories. Then they are especially curious about unusual sounds and frequently approach to chase away predators. The call works best when you hear birds giving chip calls. Chip calls are short, kiss-like sounds produced when a bird is already upset by your presence or some other disturbance.

Squeaking

Squeaking is a similar attraction technique. Try this by kissing the back of your hand to produce a prolonged squeaking sound or purchase the commercially made bird squeaker called the "Audubon Bird Call." By twisting the metal core of the bird call with varying degrees of pressure against the wooden cylinder, you can produce a variety of realistic chirps, squeaks, and trills.

Kiss your fingers or the back of your hand to produce a squeaking sound.

Not all birds are equally attracted by the pishing and squeaking techniques. Much depends on a bird's breeding condition and level of excitement when you first attempt to attract it. Some birds, such as chickadees, will give their own alarm calls if they become excited by your pishing and squeaking efforts, and these calls will help attract additional birds.

Audubon Bird Call

Mobbing Behavior

Rather than fly away from threatening predators, small birds will often swoop and dash at a predator in an effort to make it leave their territory. Mobbing behavior is commonly expressed toward owls, hawks, and snakes. Even mammal predators, such as foxes, cats, or squirrels, are usually attacked by mobs of small birds if they are discovered near active nests. You can imitate a natural predator to lure birds in for a close view.

CONSTRUCT A PAPIER-MÂCHÉ OWL

Owls provoke the most intense mobbing behaviors: just play a recording of a screech-owl call and watch the reaction. The screech-owl's trembling whistle usually attracts small birds, which flock to the sound ready to mob the owl. Even a whistle imitation of the screech owl's call will often rally a congregation of local songbirds.

You can trigger a strong mobbing reaction by playing a screech-owl recording in the presence of a papier-mâché owl model. Construct an owl by first building a chicken-wire frame. Then wrap paper strips dipped in a mixture of flour and water over the wire. Paint the owl with realistic colors, being sure to give it big yellow eyes. Mount the owl in a conspicuous place, turn on the tape recorder, and hide nearby to watch the reaction.

A real Blue Jay interacts with a papier-mâché screech-owl.

Playback Songs

Bird song alerts males of the same species that a breeding territory is occupied. If a newcomer sings within an established territory, he will soon encounter the established male. Persistent song from the challenging male is usually followed by a chase from the resident bird. You can use this chase response to lure seldom seen birds into view. Play a tape-recorded song within a bird's defended area and the territorial male will be quick to put in an appearance. Seldom-seen birds that live in the densest tangles and treetops will come into view to challenge the newcomer in their territory. Because birds cannot recognize their own voices, a singing male will come forward to defend his territory against any rival, even if the "rival" is his own recorded voice.

Tape-recorded songs are good tools to lure birds into view, but when the bird arrives, shut off the tape and just watch.

Tape-recorded songs may be made either by playing available recordings or by recording the voice of the same territorial male you are trying to observe.

Don't Interfere

While an occasional confrontation with a tape recorder probably has little effect on a breeding bird's territorial behavior, care should be taken not to use recordings in excess. Once the bird you are seeking has appeared, turn off the recorder and let the male sing his song without competition. Never use tape recordings to attract rare or endangered birds or any bird that is nesting outside its normal range. Such disturbance to a bird in precarious circumstances may threaten breeding success.

This sparrow sings from a high perch to claim ownership of his territory.

White-throated Sparrow

Treetop Birding

Not all birds are shy of people. Many land birds, such as warblers, vireos, and kinglets, will often approach surprisingly close if you meet the birds at their own level. Birds that live in treetops often are not afraid of people who climb out on a branch to meet them. Find a comfortable perch and enjoy the view.

On migration, Black-throated Blue Warblers often perch lower in trees than other warblers.

Black-throated Blue Warbler

Goldfinches are very fond of thistle seed.

American Goldfinches

Bird Gardens and Bird Feeders

Perhaps the most enjoyable way to obtain close views of wild birds is to attract them close to your home using bird feeders, water sources, and gardens that are especially attractive to birds. These attractions can be located close to windows so that your home serves as a bird blind, permitting wonderful views. Details of how to attract birds, while reducing the risk of window collisions, encounters with house cats, and other dangers, can be found in *The National Audubon Society Bird Garden* and *The National Audubon Society Bird Feeder Handbook* (see Appendix).

Eastern Bluebirds

Bluebirds and other birds often use bird-baths.

LOCATING BIRDS

Probably the greatest frustration met by beginning birders is the difficulty of finding birds with binoculars. Spotting birds with the unaided eye is one thing, but it's a very different challenge to find a bird in the narrow field of a binocular. It's difficult to remain patient when you're the only one in a group who can't find a bird. Remember that your best chance of spotting a bird is with your unaided eyes. Then lift your binoculars.

Spotting Birds

The most important tip for finding birds with binoculars is to first spot the bird with your eyes. Then, holding your head rigidly fixed to the bird, lift the binoculars to your eyes. Avoid wildly searching the trees with your binoculars. Practice spotting familiar birds that frequent feeders and live in open places before looking for birds in dense vegetation.

Practice locating stationary objects first, such as a birdhouse or tree branch. Locate large objects with your binoculars, then smaller targets.

SHARING THE DISCOVERY

If you are with a group of birders and cannot find a bird that the others see, ask for specific directions for locating the birds. Vague directions only heighten frustration and increase the chance that the bird will fly away before you see it. Encourage others to avoid such useless comments as: "There it is over there." Instead of generalizations, refer to the most obvious landmarks and narrow the field until you come to the bird. At moments of excitement, it takes as much skill to share your discovery as it does to locate birds in the first place!

The Clock Technique

- If a bird is in a tree, use the "clock" technique to describe its position. Mentally superimpose an hour hand onto the tree and use it to point to the bird. If the bird is at the edge of the tree, the system works fairly well. A bird in the top of the tree is obviously at twelve o'clock; halfway down the right side it is at three o'clock.

- If the bird is not at the edge, then the hour designation is only the first step in describing the bird's position. In addition to the hour description, one must give other pointers, such as: "Find two o'clock in the largest sycamore, then move halfway to the center of the tree. The bird is in front of the largest branch near a large woodpecker hole. See it?"

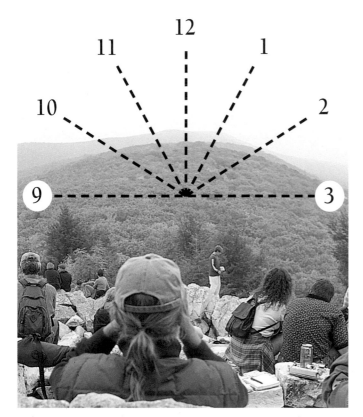

- The clock system can be superimposed on land in a horizontal position. For a land-based clock, twelve o'clock usually points north, or toward some predetermined landmark. The clock system also works for spotting birds from a moving vehicle, such as a bus or a boat. For nautical birding, the clock is viewed as it would be seen if you were above the boat looking down, with the boat in the center of the clock.

If the sun is out, a pocket mirror can be used to point out the location of birds by flashing a beam of light as a pointer. This is especially useful for pointing out nests that are high in trees or hidden in dense foliage.

LEADING A BIRD WALK

Sharing time in the field with family and friends is one of the greatest satisfactions arising from an interest in birds. A few enjoyable experiences observing birds can spark a lifetime interest, but the challenge comes in trying to make bird encounters meaningful to the novice. The sport and social elements of birding are basic to its popularity, but the catalyst that really makes it fun is an enthusiastic and considerate leader. You don't have to be an "authority" to share the excitement of identifying and watching birds. Anyone can communicate enthusiasm if he or she follows a few commonsense tips.

Plan Ahead

- Consider time of day. Most land birds are active in the early morning, rest during midday, and resume feeding in the late afternoon. After approximately 10 A.M., birds become less active and hence harder to locate; activity generally increases again after 3 P.M. This pattern is most evident in spring and early summer, when bird song and territorial defense are most conspicuous.
- Obtain permission to enter private property well ahead of time and diplomatically remind group members to respect the rights of property owners.
- Visit the intended locale the day before the field trip to see what birds you are likely to encounter. A scouting trip may also help to avoid embarrassing delays from logistical snags like closed roads, dried-up marshes, or confusing travel directions.
- Research the life histories of species that you are likely to see. If you encounter them while birding, give details about behavior, life history, and ecology. A brief investment of time reading about common birds will vitalize the trip for everyone concerned.

Consider Your Group

- The optimal size for a birding group is twelve or fewer. A group larger than twelve makes it difficult for all to see the same birds, and beginning birders are less likely to receive the attention they require from the group's leader. Whenever possible, organize car pools to minimize congestion and save fuel.
- Suggest appropriate clothes and footgear. Even if birds cooperate, wet feet or chills can easily spoil the trip. For day-long trips be certain to include an occasional rest stop.

Hiking boots

Backpack

- Ask if anyone needs assistance with binoculars, and review focusing procedures. If there are members of the group without binoculars, pair them with someone who is willing to share.

Starting the Walk

- Alert group members about some of the birds they are likely to see—but make no promises!
- Review in general terms what birds are expected to be doing at this particular season. Are they setting up territories? feeding young? getting ready to migrate?
- Ask participants to *calmly* describe the location of birds to the leader and other group members using the clock technique or landmark system.
- Explain that you as the leader should stay at the front of the group. Participants wandering ahead may flush birds that others will miss.

During the Walk

- Birding in a group has the benefit of providing many eyes and many ears to detect the movements and sounds of birds. Each person should alert the leader and other group members when he or she sees a bird. All birds are worth reporting. There is no such thing as a "trash" bird.
- Try to let everyone in the group see all birds. Certain participants will always be the last to see a bird that the rest of the group has easily located. Check to see that such individuals are spotting with their eyes, then lifting their binoculars.
- Vary the pace. When there are birds to watch, move slowly, permitting everyone to see. When birds are scarce, speed up to cover ground.
- Report field marks that you really see. Leaders frequently give the diagnostic marks for a species without actually seeing them at the time of a sighting. Unless this is clarified, beginners may question their own abilities and assume the leader has extraordinary vision or other extrasensory talents.

- Keep your binoculars up after you identify birds. What are the birds doing? What behaviors can you identify? Have the group sit at the edge of a pond or other likely birding location and practice behavior-watching (see Chapter Three). Good views are more likely to leave enduring memories than long lists of species.

Ending the Walk

- Whenever possible, reserve something special for the end of the trip—a glimpse of an active nest, an unusual bird staked out from the scouting trip, or a fine vista of the countryside.
- Pull the group together for a brief review of the birds observed. This is an appropriate time to assemble a group checklist. Suggest readings about some of the birds observed during the trip.
  - If the group comments that it's too bad the trip is over, you'll know that you've ended it at the right time.

BEGINNERS

If there are beginners in the group, they'll be just as excited about common birds as the rare ones. Don't turn your bird walk into a search for rarities. All birds deserve attention; the challenge to the experienced birder is to maintain enthusiasm about the thousandth Barn Swallow or Song Sparrow. Remember that there are likely to be people in your group who are seeing the bird for the first time—try to remember your first encounter.

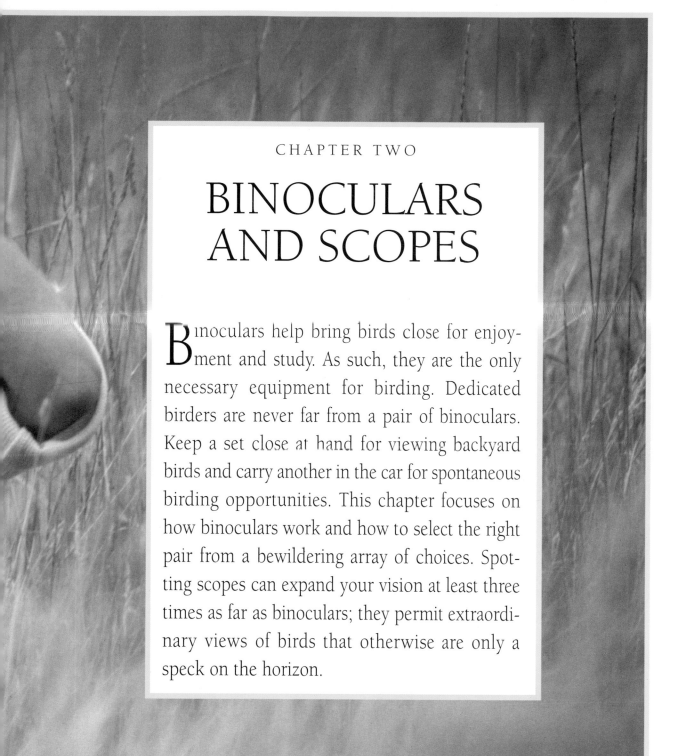

CHAPTER TWO

BINOCULARS AND SCOPES

Binoculars help bring birds close for enjoyment and study. As such, they are the only necessary equipment for birding. Dedicated birders are never far from a pair of binoculars. Keep a set close at hand for viewing backyard birds and carry another in the car for spontaneous birding opportunities. This chapter focuses on how binoculars work and how to select the right pair from a bewildering array of choices. Spotting scopes can expand your vision at least three times as far as binoculars; they permit extraordinary views of birds that otherwise are only a speck on the horizon.

How Binoculars Work

Binoculars are the most important tools for watching birds, but the selection of the "right" set can be a bewildering task when you consider such features as power, coating, field of view, size, and weight. The selection task is especially difficult because binoculars that look similar from the outside may vary in price, anywhere from $40 to $1,200 (U.S.). Here are some tips to keep in mind when making your selection.

Power

Examine the flat upper surface of the binoculars' housing and you'll note two numbers, such as 7x35 or 8x40. The first of the two numbers designates the binoculars' power. Eight-power binoculars make subjects appear eight times larger than they would without magnification. Most birders use 8x binoculars, but some prefer binoculars as powerful as 10x. The latter are especially useful for viewing birds that are likely to be in the open (where light is bright) or for watching birds that are not very active, such as hawks, seabirds, waterfowl, and shorebirds. The higher the magnification, the more difficult it is to hold binoculars steady—high magnifications exaggerate movements of the observer. Consider your ability to hold binoculars steady; if you have a trembling hand, stay away from binoculars greater than 8x.

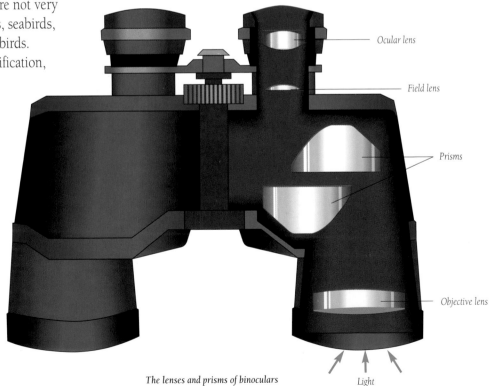

Ocular lens

Field lens

Prisms

Objective lens

Light

The lenses and prisms of binoculars

Light-gathering Capacity

Light enters binoculars through the objective lenses. The diameter of these lenses is the second of the numbers on the binoculars, as in the 7x35 designation. Accordingly, 7x50 binoculars have larger objective lenses without a gain in magnification. The advantage of the larger objective lens is its greater light-gathering capacity.

The exit pupil is the best measure of the binoculars' brightness. You can easily see the exit pupil by holding the binoculars at arm's distance and looking into the eyepieces. Ideally, the exit pupil should appear as a brilliant, clear circle. While binoculars with larger exit pupils generally offer brighter images and better color, these advantages are not achieved without trade-offs. The principal drawback is additional weight and oversized housing necessary to support the larger and heavier optics.

Check this table to determine which exit pupil size meets your needs:

Exit Pupil Size	Appropriate Situations
2-4 mm	Bright-light (open land, mountain vistas, shorelines)
4-5 mm	Shaded areas; boating
Over 5 mm	Dusk; dawn; brighter images at all times

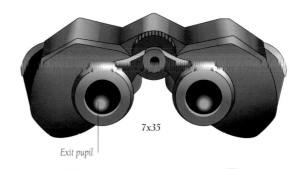

7x35

Exit pupil

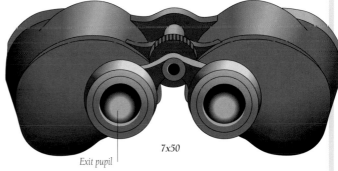

7x50

Exit pupil

To find the exit pupil size, divide the size of the objective lens by the magnification number. Thus, the 7x35 binocular has an exit pupil of 5 mm, as compared to the brighter 7.1 mm exit pupil of the 7x50 binocular.

Birders looking for binoculars to use on boats will find that an exit pupil of at least 5 mm offers a distinct advantage. When motion causes your binoculars to move in all directions around your eyes, you may experience image blackouts as the exit pupil moves away from the pupil of your eye. In bright daylight, when your eye has a pupil opening of 2 mm, a binocular with a 5 mm exit pupil provides a 3 mm leeway to adjust to the movement.

Just as the large eyes of an owl gather enough light to permit nocturnal vision, binoculars with large objective lenses offer an advantage for bird-watching at dusk and dawn or in dark habitats such as forests.

Coated Optics

Light entering the objective lens must pass through as many as eight pieces of optical glass in each barrel. At each glass surface some light will be reflected backward rather than passing through the binoculars. The optics of well-made binoculars are coated with an even film of magnesium fluoride that helps deliver more than 90 percent of the light gathered by the objective lenses. Without coating, binoculars may reflect away from your eyes up to 60 percent of the light entering the objective lenses.

    Although most manufacturers coat the exterior lenses, some inexpensive binoculars may not have all interior optics coated. Even though some manufacturers state that their binoculars have "fully coated optics," it's best to check for yourself. Hold the binocular under a fluorescent light and look into the objective lenses. Search for purple-violet or amber reflections on all interior optics. White reflections are evidence of uncoated optics.

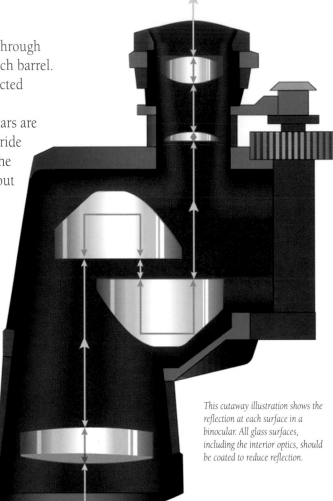

This cutaway illustration shows the reflection at each surface in a binocular. All glass surfaces, including the interior optics, should be coated to reduce reflection.

BACKLIT SUBJECTS

Coated optics are also an aid when looking at backlit subjects. Without coating, light reflects within binoculars, causing annoying glare. Even with coated optics, you should never look directly at the sun because intense magnification of sunlight can cause eye damage.

Here, the exit pupil on the left is blocked by gray at the edges, indicating that some light is being blocked by inferior internal optics. The exit pupil on the right is not blocked.

Light Gathering

When making your selection, keep in mind that light-gathering quality is not determined solely by the size of the objective lenses. Certain features of lower priced binoculars may cancel the light-gathering advantages of large binoculars with out-sized objective lenses. Carefully examine the edges of the exit pupil to see if it is a complete, bright circle or if the edges are shaded gray, resulting in a bright central square.

Field of View

Field of view is the width of the image you see while looking through the binoculars. It is usually measured as the width of area visible at 1,000 yards from the observer—for example, 400 feet at 1,000 yards. Sometimes the field of view is expressed in degrees, usually engraved on the surface of the housing near the eyepiece. If so, you can calculate field of view by multiplying the number of degrees by 52.5 (the number of feet in 1 degree at 1,000 yards). Thus, the field of view for a 7-degree binocular would be 7 x 52.5 = 367.5 feet at 1,000 yards.

The wider the field of view, the easier it is to locate birds with your binoculars. Wide-angle binoculars are of special value to beginning bird-watchers, since the larger field makes it easier to find birds—especially flying birds or those inhabiting dense vegetation. Extra–wide-angle binoculars expand the field by increasing the size and number of lenses in the ocular system. The additional optics increases the cost of the binoculars and makes them bulky to hold. Since it's difficult to produce binoculars that have sharp images across the entire field, beware of low-cost binoculars claiming a wide field of view. They are probably sharp only in the center of the field. With experience, most bird-watchers find that a standard field of view (obtained with most 7x35, 8x40, and 10x50 binoculars) is usually adequate and that there is little need to invest in extra–wide-angle binoculars.

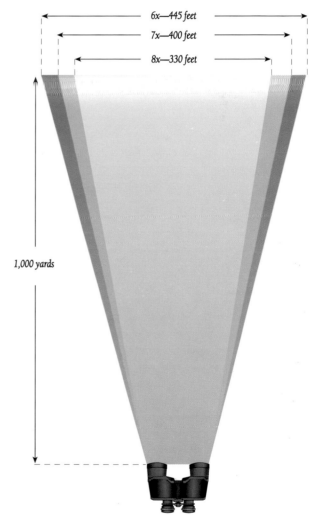

The field of view is the width of the image you see through the binoculars. This illustration shows the field of view at 1,000 yards for 6x, 7x, and 8x binoculars. As magnification increases, the field of view decreases.

Resolution

High-quality optical glass may cost more than $300 (U.S.) a pound, and each lens and prism must be professionally ground and mounted with expert precision. High-quality binoculars are finely crafted instruments. Attention to such details as balancing and matching lenses is basic to the production of the best products. Some manufacturers cut corners throughout production, especially by using low-quality glass and less of it. For these reasons, the price of binoculars is one of the best indicators of quality. High-priced binoculars usually have better optics, resulting in sharper images and less eyestrain.

High-quality binoculars have crisp images from the center to the edge of the field of view. You can check this by looking at a map or newspaper tacked to a wall. Stand back about 25 feet and see if you can read the print in both the center and edge of the field.

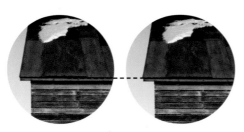

Binoculars in alignment

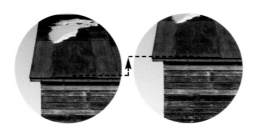

Binoculars out of alignment

Check the alignment of new binoculars by looking at the roof of a house through them, then moving the binoculars about eight inches away from your eyes to create two separate images. If the binoculars are in alignment, the horizontal line of the roof should be at the same level in both fields.

Alignment

The twin-barrel design of binoculars makes them vulnerable to loss of alignment. When binoculars are functioning properly, both sides focus on the same field of view; however, if binoculars receive a sharp jolt, they can easily be thrown out of alignment, and the two fields will no longer overlap. If you look through binoculars that are out of alignment, your eyes will attempt to bring the two views together. If alignment is far off, you'll see double images, and the subject will look blurry. Binoculars that are only slightly out of alignment may be more of a problem because your eyes will strain to bring the two images together; the result will be fatigued eyes and a headache.

Low-priced binoculars are more likely to develop alignment problems than high-priced models; prisms and lenses in cut-rate models may be glued in place rather than securely strapped by metal brackets. Temperature changes or slight jars can throw them out of alignment. Realigning binoculars is not a simple task, because they must be taken apart by an experienced technician and recalibrated using special equipment. It may be less expensive to replace a pair of binoculars than to have them realigned.

Selecting Binoculars

- Compare binoculars of the same magnification by holding one atop the other. Alternately look through each binocular, comparing for brightness and clarity. Compare the best from your first comparison with a third pair. Continue this process of elimination until you've examined what's available.
- Holding the binoculars at arm's distance, check the exit pupils to see if they are blocked by gray shadows at the edges. Nearly all binoculars under $100 (U.S.) will show the gray border obstructing the exit pupil.
- Look into the objective lenses to see that surfaces are coated with an even purple-violet or amber hue without white reflections from inside. Examine the objective and ocular lenses for scratches.
- Be sure that all mechanical parts move smoothly and that the bridge supporting the barrels does not wobble.
- Check alignment by looking at a rooftop or horizontal power line. Examine the print on a sign to see if you can read the lettering at the edge of the field as well as at the center.

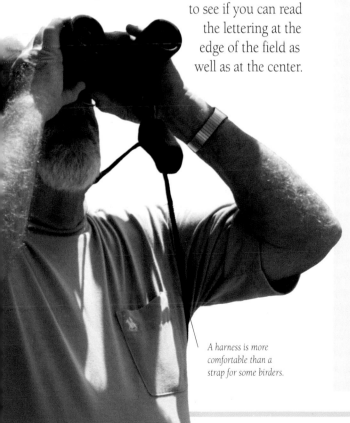

A harness is more comfortable than a strap for some birders.

- Look at the edge of a backlit sign or building to see if there is a band of bright color fringing the object. This is the result of an inferior lens system unable to bring light of different wavelengths together at the same point.
- After narrowing the field, select the highest-priced binoculars you can afford. Higher price means sharper images, brighter colors, less chance of alignment problems, and a longer binocular life. Lower priced binoculars require compromises, but even an inexpensive pair will launch your bird-watching experiences.

Focusing Your Binoculars

Stand about thirty feet from a sign with clear lettering and follow these steps:

- Note that the two binocular barrels pivot on the hinge post, permitting the eyepieces to fit over your eyes comfortably. Spread the barrels as wide as you can. Hold the binoculars at eye level and press the barrels together until the two images converge into one.
- Turn the center focus wheel, moving both eyepieces to the maximum distance from the body of the binocular. Note that only one of the eyepieces has calibrations on it (usually the right eyepiece). Turn the calibrated eyepiece counterclockwise, moving it as far from the body of the binoculars as possible. Both eyepieces should be out of focus.
- Facing the sign with eyes shut, lift the binoculars into position. With your left eye open, turn the center focus wheel until the lettering comes into sharp focus. To be sure you have the sharpest focus, pass the sharpest point and then back up to find it.
- Shut your left eye and with your right eye open, turn the right eyepiece in a clockwise direction, bringing the lettering into focus. Pass the point of sharp focus and then back up to where the lettering is sharpest. Now the binoculars should be in perfect focus.
- Note the right eyepiece setting, as it is now adjusted to your eyes. The only reason for it to change would be to accommodate a change in vision. After the right eyepiece is set, you need only adjust the center wheel to focus both eyepieces.

TYPES OF BINOCULARS

When choosing binoculars, first select the general type before considering specific models. The following pages cover some types of binoculars and discuss the pros and cons of each style. Once you have selected a category of binoculars, price will be one of the best general measures of quality, durability, clarity, and color resolution.

Center-focus

Individual-focus

Center-focus Versus Individual-focus Binoculars

Most birders prefer center-focus binoculars to individual-focus eyepieces because the center-focus design permits the viewer to focus on birds that are as close as ten feet. In contrast, individual-focus binoculars must be reset when looking at subjects closer than about thirty feet, which makes them awkward for watching most land birds. The individual-focus design is better suited for use on boats, where birds seldom come closer than thirty feet; the sealed design gives important protection from rain and water spray.

Roof-prism binoculars

Roof-prism Binoculars

Roof-prism binoculars have straight barrels, a feature achieved by placing the two prisms in each barrel close together. Roof-prism binoculars offer several advantages over the standard (Porro prism) design. They have excellent resolution without sacrificing brightness or field of view. Internal focusing mechanics permit focusing without the eyepieces moving in and out from the binocular body—a feature that protects internal optics from moisture and dirt. Roof-prism binoculars do not offer the depth perception of the standard prism design, nor do they focus as closely. Their principal drawback is the high cost for repairs and initial purchase price, which may exceed $1,000 (U.S.).

Roof-prism binoculars have straight barrels.

Mini Binoculars

There are many palm-sized binocular midgets available, but these generally offer extremely narrow fields of view. The principal trade-off is light: with objective lens sizes no larger than 30 mm, these tiny binoculars are most useful in bright-light situations. If you purchase mini binoculars, choose from the high-end price range ($300-$500 [U.S.]). A few models at this price range can deliver images of sharpness comparable to that of standard (Porro prism) and roof-prism binoculars.

Models within the upper price range are finely crafted instruments containing more than a hundred individual mechanical parts and sixteen optical components. Tested to withstand the rigors of temperature extremes and sudden jolts, they provide a viable binocular option to the birder already encumbered by bulky camera gear, tape recording equipment, and field guides.

Mini binoculars

Rubber eyecups

Binoculars for eye-glass wearers

Porro-prism binoculars have offset barrels.

Binoculars for Eyeglass Wearers

People who wear eyeglasses should focus their binoculars through their glasses so that they can use the binoculars without first removing their eyeglasses. This creates a special problem, however, because eyeglasses block binoculars from close contact with the eye, and the extra distance between eye and lens reduces the field of view. Shallow eyecups on your binoculars can help solve this problem. Some binoculars are available with interchangeable shallow and deep eyecups. Rubber eyecups, which roll down for eyeglass users, or snap-in eyecups are the best solution to this problem. Binoculars that are specially designed for eyeglass wearers often have the letter B (referring to low eye-relief) following the numbers of the objective lens—for example, 8x42B.

BINOCULAR CARE

Binoculars used for birding face many hazards to which binoculars used at opera houses and football stadiums are rarely subjected. In addition to being able to withstand precipitation and highly corrosive salt spray, bird-watching binoculars should be rugged enough to accompany birders up rocky slopes, in and out of boats, and through wet and dry bird habitats. Center-focus binoculars (the preferred type for birding) are vulnerable to water and dirt, which may enter through the focusing apparatus. High-end binoculars are fully sealed to exclude water and dust.

Cleaning Binoculars

Dirty binoculars provide neither sharp detail nor crisp colors. Binoculars should be cleaned frequently, following these suggestions:

- Hold binoculars upside down so that dirt will fall away from the lens surface. Then thoroughly use a camera-quality blower brush (or compressed air) to dislodge grit and dust from lenses. Unless removed, dirt will easily scratch the lens and its coating.
- Fold a piece of lens-cleaning tissue so that it is at least four layers thick. This prevents oil from your fingers soaking through the tissue and onto the lens surface. Use a circular movement to gently wipe all lens surfaces.
- If there is a film of oil on the lens, put a drop of lens cleaner on the tissue and repeat the circular wiping movement.
- Look for dirt on internal optics by holding the binoculars up to a light, while looking into the objective lenses. Never attempt to open binoculars, since alignment is easily disrupted. Despite the expense, you should leave internal cleaning to the professionals.

Multipurpose cleaning cloth

Tips to Extend the Life of Your Binoculars

PROTECTING THEM

When performing active maneuvers, such as jumping across a ditch, climbing a rock slope, or getting into a boat, tuck the binoculars inside your jacket or secure them under your arm.

A sturdy strap will keep binoculars secure around your neck.

HANDLE THEM GENTLY

Don't stroll through the woods swinging your binoculars by the strap. When in the field, always keep them around your neck or over your shoulder.

KEEP BINOCULARS DRY

Keep your binoculars under cover if it starts raining. Water can leak into the housing, carrying with it dirt that will stain the internal optics. Rain guards offer some protection during light rains and drizzles, but they are not adequate protection for heavy rains. If your binoculars "steam up" on the inside, set them in a warm, dry place; they are likely to dry out in a couple of days. Otherwise, fungus may start growing on the lens coating. Some high-end binoculars are waterproof—a feature that is worth the investment.

SAVING WET BINOCULARS

If binoculars fall into freshwater, have them professionally cleaned as soon as possible to avoid rusting. If they are dropped into salt water, rinse them thoroughly in freshwater, seal them in a plastic bag, and rush them to a professional service department within three days of the soaking. If the water-soaked binoculars were inexpensive to start with, you might as well buy a new pair; the repair charge will probably exceed the purchase price.

BINOCULARS IN THE CAR

When driving a car, don't leave your binoculars on the seat because a quick stop will send them flying forward. Be certain not to leave your binoculars sitting exposed in the car, especially on a hot summer day. If thieves don't find them, the sun may soften the lens coatings, causing them to crack and separate from the lenses.

Insuring Field Equipment

Considering the perils to which bird-watching binoculars and other field equipment are exposed, it's a good idea to insure them against damage or loss. If you have homeowner's or renter's insurance, ask your agent to extend the policy to give all-risk worldwide coverage to your binoculars, scopes, cameras, and other equipment. The basic policy will insure equipment at home and in the field against theft; for a few dollars extra, the all-risk policy will cover your equipment if it should be damaged, lost, dropped overboard, or run over by a passing tractor.

SPOTTING SCOPES

Spotting scopes provide the magnification necessary to see distant birds and to admire detail at closer ranges. Scopes are most frequently used to watch waterfowl, shorebirds, and hawks that live in expansive habitats such as wetlands and open fields. Scopes can also permit full-field, intimate views of birds already at close range. Such views frequently reveal the intricate beauty of a bird's plumage and permit the observation of behavior that might otherwise go unseen.

Magnification

The problems that accompany power increases in binoculars also apply to spotting scopes. High powers magnify the air as well as the subject, often producing hazy images or distracting shimmering from heat vibrations over water and flat expanses such as farmlands. Under good observation conditions, the large objective lens and the use of a tripod permit telescopes to greatly magnify images beyond what you would see with binoculars.

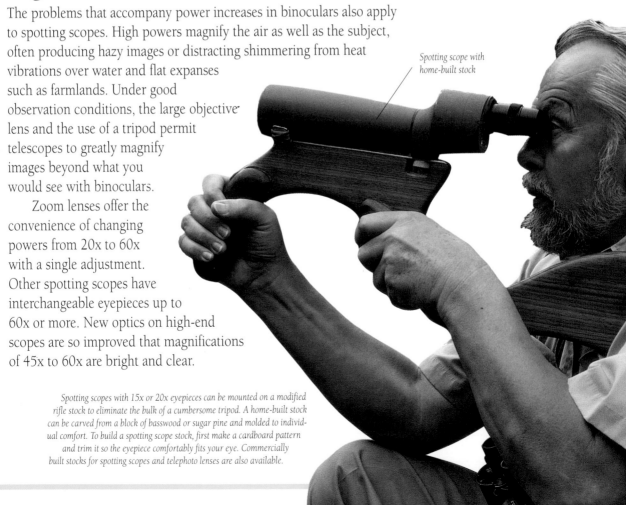

Spotting scope with home-built stock

Zoom lenses offer the convenience of changing powers from 20x to 60x with a single adjustment. Other spotting scopes have interchangeable eyepieces up to 60x or more. New optics on high-end scopes are so improved that magnifications of 45x to 60x are bright and clear.

Spotting scopes with 15x or 20x eyepieces can be mounted on a modified rifle stock to eliminate the bulk of a cumbersome tripod. A home-built stock can be carved from a block of basswood or sugar pine and molded to individual comfort. To build a spotting scope stock, first make a cardboard pattern and trim it so the eyepiece comfortably fits your eye. Commercially built stocks for spotting scopes and telephoto lenses are also available.

Selecting a Scope

- Consider future use. Spotting scopes are rugged field instruments of moderate cost that are best used just for watching birds. If you intend to use the scope frequently for photography and/or astronomy, then the more expensive (and delicate) reflector telescopes may be the answer.
- For use on a rifle stock, stick with a 20x objective. For use on a tripod, zoom lenses that vary in power from 20x to 60x are worth the expense, as the lower magnifications are good for scanning and the upper range is good for detailed views.
- Don't buy a cheap telescope. Inexpensive scopes deliver fuzzy, distorted images, manufacturing defects will lead to the early demise of your instrument and disappointing field performances.
- Select a rigid tripod with as few leg adjustments as possible. In general, the fewer leg adjustments, the better.

Scope

Flip-locks

Tripod

If the scope will be shared by members of a group or used at higher magnifications, it should be mounted on a tripod. Some tripods are clumsy to use because they may have as many as nine different locks and clamps controlling the extension of the legs; not infrequently, the last leg is secured just as the bird leaves. The most efficient tripods are those that feature "flip locks." These tripods are easy to operate because once the legs are released, they fall to their own level and are locked in place by locks located on the legs.

Small Reflector Telescopes

Small telescopes are deluxe aids for watching birds. They can also double as acceptable telephoto lenses in the 1,000 to 2,000 mm range and are ideal for astronomical use. The principal advantage of the reflector telescope is that it offers significantly greater magnification than a spotting scope without serious loss of light and sharpness. Scanning is accomplished through the built-in viewfinder, which provides magnifications of 4x or 8x, depending on the eyepiece used. Small flip levers engage either the medium- or high-power magnifications. Several eyepieces are available, but the 32 mm eyepiece is the most useful focal length, since it permits magnifications of 40x and 64x that are a marvel of brilliance and sharpness even under the darker conditions of dawn and dusk.

The greatest drawback to small telescopes of the mixed lens/mirror design is the high purchase price, which may exceed $3,000 (U.S.). For birders who can afford them, they offer an unequaled extension of vision for watching birds.

CHAPTER THREE

OBSERVING BIRDS

Watching behavior adds a new dimension to birding because it shifts the emphasis from identifying species to observing individual birds. In order to survive, birds have evolved specific behaviors to find food, secure a mate, and raise young while maintaining vigorous health and plumage. Not only does each species have its own set of special behaviors, but every bird has a unique personality. Even the most common birds can be entertaining as they reveal their repertoire of behaviors.

WATCHING BIRD BEHAVIOR

After you've established their identities, keep watching and you will find that birds are usually busy with a variety of interesting behaviors. New bird species are seldom discovered, but even the most abundant species perform activities that are either unknown or seldom described. Even the most common activities, such as feeding and nesting behaviors, need further attention. The next time you go birding, focus your attention on bird actions and see how many of the following behaviors you can observe.

Body-Care Behaviors

Birds are covered with thousands of feathers, and usually molt once or twice a year. Replacing worn feathers costs birds much energy and sometimes makes them vulnerable to predators. To extend the life of feathers and minimize the need for replacement, birds spend much of their day maintaining their plumage. Birds ranging in size from eagles to hummingbirds will care for their feathers in surprisingly similar ways, yet careful observation will often show subtle differences among closely related species. Start watching for different body-care behaviors among backyard and feeder birds; most behaviors in this category are easily observed at any time of the year.

Brown Pelican

A gland located at the base of the tail produces oil.

Eastern Bluebird

PREENING
Birds must devote a large portion of each day to arranging their plumage. Preening typically consists of sliding each feather through the beak, nibbling the feather from base to tip so that separated feather vanes are zipped together.

BATHING

Bathing helps to reorganize the plumage more than to clean it and is usually followed by active preening and spreading of oil from the preen gland. Most landbirds and waterbirds bathe. Watch carefully to see which parts of the body are wet first, and see if you can discover a predictable pattern.

American Crow

ANTING

Many land birds sit on active ant colonies permitting the ants to roam freely through their plumage. Some species lift their feathers, permitting the ants to crawl to their skin, while others pick up the ants and, with a squeeze, tuck them into their plumage. The behavior is little understood, but it may help to remove ectoparasites by treating the feathers with formic acid from the ants.

Tufted Puffin

Bathing is important both to the organization of plumage and to the cleaning of it.

DUSTING

Birds of dry habitats perform bathing behaviors in depressions scooped out of dusty soil. Dusting may help birds control ectoparasites, such as feather mites, and remove excess oils from feathers. Some birds, such as hawks, kinglets, and sparrows, bathe in both dust and water.

Willow Ptarmigan

OILING

Most birds keep their feathers lubricated and waterproofed by spreading oil from their uropygial gland. The gland, located at the base of the tail, is usually stimulated by a squeeze from the bird's beak. The oil is spread onto the plumage and worked into the feathers by preening.

Birds clean their beaks by wiping one side and then the other.

Black-capped Chickadee

BILL WIPING

After eating, land birds usually clean excess food from their beaks by wiping one side of the beak and then the other against a convenient perch. Bill wiping is commonly expressed at moments of tension, even if the bird has not eaten recently.

FEATHER RUFFLING AND FLUFFING

Feather ruffling is a cooling behavior that permits warm air near the skin surface to escape when feathers are raised. Although similar in appearance to ruffling, feather fluffing occurs during cold temperatures and conserves body heat by increasing the insulating function of the plumage.

Song Sparrow

Fluffing increases the insulation value of plumage.

PANTING

Birds pant to cool themselves when frightened or overheated. Panting is usually accompanied by gular fluttering, a rapid quivering of the throat that promotes cooling.

Panting helps to cool overheated birds.

Mute Swan

Great Blue Heron

FEATHER SETTLING

When arranging their plumage, birds raise their feathers, shake their bodies, and stretch their wings before settling the feathers back into place. Unlike feather-ruffling or feather-fluffing postures, which are prolonged responses to temperature stresses, feather settling is not temperature related and lasts only a few seconds.

Sandhill Crane

STRETCHING

Birds frequently stretch the limbs of one side of their bodies. Typically, the wing, leg, and half the tail are extended out and backward. After the stretch is completed, a bird will frequently repeat the process with the other side of its body.

Birds often stretch their wings, first one side and then the other.

American Oystercatcher

SCRATCHING

Birds scratch with their feet in predictable ways. Most perching birds scratch over their wings, but some closely related species scratch in surprisingly different, yet also predictable, ways.

Many birds lay their heads on their backs when sleeping.

Mallard

SLEEPING

Most birds have a headless appearance when sleeping because they lay their heads on their backs, tucking their beaks under their shoulder feathers. Birds that are resting but not sleeping may shut their eyes, but they do not usually put their beaks on their backs.

Birds often yawn before resting or sleeping.

Bird Behavior Versus Human Behavior

When watching bird behavior, consider that bird senses are fundamentally different from our own. For example, most birds have a poor or nonexistent sense of smell but keen vision that can resolve details at two to three times the distance achieved by humans, and a sense of orientation that is nothing short of astounding. Research demonstrates that birds can orient by star patterns and magnetic fields and that they are capable of hearing infrasounds—extremely low-frequency vibrations—which may give them the ability to hear wind moving through mountains and ocean breakers hundreds of miles away.

Since birds experience the world with senses that are usually keener than our own and often respond instinctively, it is essential to avoid assigning human motives and values to bird behavior. Birds are neither good nor bad, and despite perceived similarities in their behavior to that of humans, they are never sneaky, happy, or sad. Such descriptions are totally inappropriate for describing bird behavior.

Feeding Strategies

Although special adaptations set limits on the kinds of foods birds can eat, most birds consume a surprising variety of food, frequently switching feeding strategies depending on what foods are available or their nutritional needs for a certain season. Even birds that have beaks especially adapted for specific foods will often opt for an alternative. Hummingbirds, for example, frequently prey upon the small insects they find in flowers, although their primary food is flower nectar. Grosbeaks, which normally use their massive beaks to crack seeds, primarily feed their young a diet of easy-to-digest, high-protein insects. Any dramatic changes in diet usually require impressive shifts in feeding strategies.

HAWKING
Searching for food while perched, then flying out to capture flying insects, and returning to the same or a nearby perch. Examples: kingbirds, waxwings, and Great Crested Flycatchers.

Great Crested Flycatcher

Birds carrying food in their beaks are usually on their way to feed their young.

Black-capped Chickadee

HOVER GLEANING
Hovering while searching for insects or other small invertebrates on tree leaves, a tree trunk, or other surfaces. Examples: kinglets, phoebes.

Say's Phoebe

PERCH AND SALLY GLEANING

Perch gleaning involves searching for prey while perched in a tree or shrub and capturing insects or other small invertebrates, such as spiders, mites, or ticks, without flying from the searching position. Examples: most wood warblers, chickadees, titmice. Sally gleaning, on the other hand, refers to searching for food while perched, then flying out to snatch an insect or other small invertebrate prey off a distant surface, such as leaves or a tree trunk. Examples: Red-eyed Vireos; Least, Acadian, and Willow Flycatchers.

Western Sandpipers

CHISELING

Pounding on a tree trunk creates a cavity and access to prey. Pounding also disturbs insects and other small invertebrates, making them come to the surface. Example: woodpeckers.

Yellow-bellied Sapsucker

Prey may lie under a layer of leaves.

Ruffed Grouse

PROBING

Reaching into tree bark, soil, or mud with the beak in search of prey. Examples: Brown Creepers, nuthatches, woodcocks, dowitchers, sandpipers.

LEAF TOSSING

Scratching at the leaf litter layer with the feet looking for prey under leaves. Examples: towhees, Fox Sparrows, Ruffed Grouse.

Barn Swallow

Some birds capture insects in flight.

SWEEPING

Searching for insects in the air and capturing them in flight with a wide-open mouth. Examples: swallows, swifts, nighthawks.

Microhabitats

Carefully observe opportunistic foragers, such as gulls, crows, and starlings, which use their all-purpose beaks and bodies to consume a remarkable variety of plant and animal foods. Also watch for subtle differences in the places birds forage. Studies of warbler feeding behavior show that several species can forage on the same tree without competing for food. Likewise, shorebird species find different foods at various distances from the shoreline, just as woodpeckers find different prey in the same tree by chiseling holes of various depths. On your next birding trip, see how many feeding microhabitats you can observe.

POUNCING
Flying to the
ground to
capture prey.
Examples: owls,
hawks, eagles,
bluebirds.

SHELL SMASHING
Dropping clams, mussels,
or turtles from the air onto
land surfaces to crack the
shells and obtain the
contents. Examples: gulls,
crows, eagles.

Great Black-backed Gull

*Some birds drop shells
or crabs, which may
crack upon landing.*

Barn Owl

Roseate Spoonbill

Peregrine Falcon

SIFTING
Straining animals and plants from mud or water.
Examples: flamingos, spoonbills, shovelers.

STOOPING
Dropping at great speed in
pursuit of flying birds or
insect prey. Example: falcons.

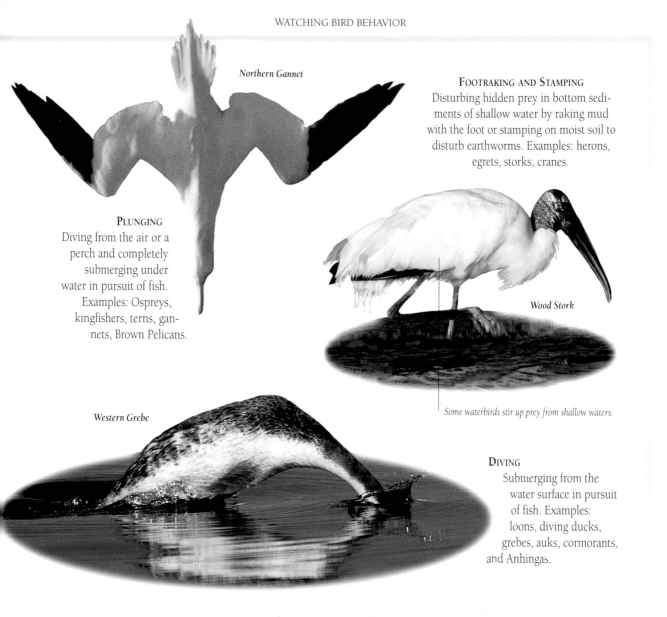

Northern Gannet

FOOTRAKING AND STAMPING
Disturbing hidden prey in bottom sediments of shallow water by raking mud with the foot or stamping on moist soil to disturb earthworms. Examples: herons, egrets, storks, cranes.

PLUNGING
Diving from the air or a perch and completely submerging under water in pursuit of fish. Examples: Ospreys, kingfishers, terns, gannets, Brown Pelicans.

Wood Stork

Some waterbirds stir up prey from shallow waters.

Western Grebe

DIVING
Submerging from the water surface in pursuit of fish. Examples: loons, diving ducks, grebes, auks, cormorants, and Anhingas.

STALKING
Standing, walking, or wading in search of fish, insects, or other prey, or snatching animals from shallow water or the land surface. Examples: herons, gulls, plovers, robins, thrushes, larks, dippers.

Tricolored Heron

PIRACY
Stealing food from other birds.
Examples: Herring Gulls,
frigatebirds, Bald Eagles.

Frigatebirds

Canada Goose

American Wigeons

DABBLING
Tipping tail up and stretching downward
without completely submerging to reach
the bottom vegetation of shallow waters.
Examples: swans, Mallards, and other
dabbling ducks.

GRAZING
Biting off or pulling up rooted land vegetation.
Example: Canada Geese.

*Scavenging birds feed on
carrion on the ground*

SCAVENGING
Consuming dead animal matter, usually
searching from the air and then feeding on the ground or water. Examples: vultures, crows, gulls.

Black Vulture

Nesting material

Some birds steal nesting material as well as food from one another

NECTAR HOVERING
Hovering at flowers to feed on nectar.
Example: hummingbirds.

Ruby-throated Hummingbird

Dark-eyed Junco

Birds on the ground peck for seeds or fruit.

PRUNING
Nipping off and consuming twigs and buds. Examples: Pine Grosbeaks, grouse, and ptarmigans.

Willow Ptarmigan

PECKING
Searching on the ground and picking up loose seeds or consuming fallen fruit. Examples: geese, pheasants, juncos, sparrows.

American Goldfinch

PLUCKING
Removing fruit and seeds from vegetation. Examples: American Robins, Cedar Waxwings, Purple Finches, goldfinches, Bohemian Waxwings.

Herring Gull

SURFACE FEEDING
Capturing prey by skimming or plucking food from the surface of the water. Examples: Black Skimmers, petrels, frigatebirds, gulls, phalaropes.

Social Displays

Social displays include all interactions among birds of the same species. Certain displays, such as mobbing and flocking, appear among a great variety of birds, while other displays, such as song and courtship performances, are unique for each species. Most social displays are linked in some way to the reproductive cycle and are greatly influenced by seasons of the year. When watching social displays, look for ritualized body-care behaviors, such as preening and feather-ruffling postures. Such behaviors are often incorporated into courtship performances, but they can surface at seemingly inappropriate times, when the bird is under stress, and are then known as "displacement activities" (such as bill wiping).

Birds often mob predators or chase them from their territory.

CAUTION DISPLAYS

When approaching the nest, birds often assume a nervous caution display consisting of searching in an erect posture, tail flicking, and bill wiping. The duration of caution displays is greatly influenced by the presence of predators and human observers.

Purple Martin

MOBBING

When a predator, such as a fox, snake, or owl, is discovered, birds of many species will join together to chase the predator from the vicinity.

THREAT AND APPEASEMENT DISPLAYS

Birds frequently exhibit threat displays when defending feeding or nesting territories from intruders. Common elements of the threat display include gaping (opening beak as if to bite) and wing opening and head lowering (as if to attack). Actual fights among birds are rare because of the appeasement posture when retreating from a threat. A bird in an appeasement posture frequently hunches its shoulders, lowers its beak, and turns away from the threatening bird. Watch for threat and appeasement displays at feeding stations.

Pine Siskins

Birds maintain a small distance from each other even when flocking together.

Bohemian Waxwings

FLOCKING

Many species flock together prior to and during migration. Other species roost together at night, gaining protection from predators and perhaps communicating information about available food supplies. Even in dense roosting flocks, birds always maintain an individual distance of at least several inches from the nearest bird.

Killdeer

FREEZING

Ground-nesting birds, such as woodcocks, grouse, and certain sparrows, rely on their camouflage and remaining still, or freezing, when a predator threatens. If a bird flushes from underfoot, be careful, since its nest is likely nearby.

DISTRACTION DISPLAYS

When the nest or young are threatened, some parent birds experience a conflict between attacking and fleeing. Birds nesting on the ground in open habitats frequently respond with a compromise behavior called the broken-wing act, in which the parent flees the nest but flutters and calls as if it is mortally crippled. The predator usually follows the distressed parent only to find the adult "recovers" at a safe distance from the nest. Birds nesting on the ground in dense, grassy habitats may perform a similar distraction display called rodent running, in which they creep along the ground away from the nest like a vulnerable rodent.

CALLS AND SONGS

Given by both sexes, calls are short, nonmusical vocalizations that function to communicate information about daily activities, such as feeding, flocking, migration, and alarm. Songs, on the other hand, are used by the male to attract a mate and to alert males of the same species that the territory is occupied. Each species has a unique song. With few exceptions, female birds do not sing.

Dickcissel

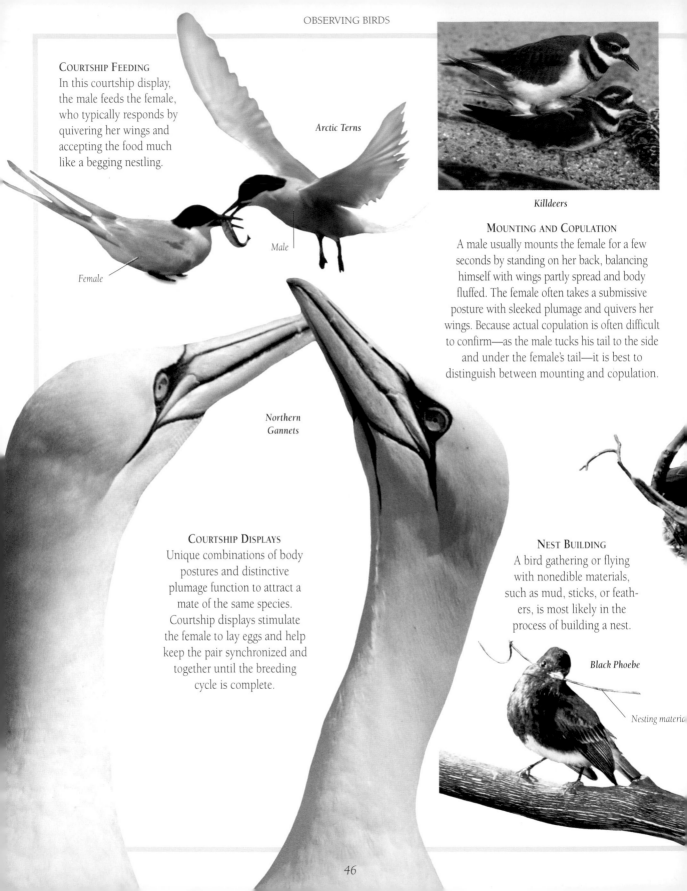

COURTSHIP FEEDING
In this courtship display, the male feeds the female, who typically responds by quivering her wings and accepting the food much like a begging nestling.

Arctic Terns

Male

Female

Killdeers

MOUNTING AND COPULATION
A male usually mounts the female for a few seconds by standing on her back, balancing himself with wings partly spread and body fluffed. The female often takes a submissive posture with sleeked plumage and quivers her wings. Because actual copulation is often difficult to confirm—as the male tucks his tail to the side and under the female's tail—it is best to distinguish between mounting and copulation.

Northern Gannets

COURTSHIP DISPLAYS
Unique combinations of body postures and distinctive plumage function to attract a mate of the same species. Courtship displays stimulate the female to lay eggs and help keep the pair synchronized and together until the breeding cycle is complete.

NEST BUILDING
A bird gathering or flying with nonedible materials, such as mud, sticks, or feathers, is most likely in the process of building a nest.

Black Phoebe

Nesting material

Piping Plover

Egg

INCUBATION

Most birds incubate their eggs against a patch of skin, called the brood patch, bared by molting during the breeding season. Incubation takes about two weeks for small land birds and about three weeks for shorebirds.

EGG TURNING

Parent birds must turn the eggs several times each day for the embryos to develop successfully. The eggs are usually turned by placing the bill on the far side of the egg and lifting, thus turning the egg in place.

Black-necked Stilt

Canada Goose

Nestling warmed by mother

House Wren

CARRYING FOOD

When you see birds carrying food, it is usually evidence that they have a nearby nest with young.

BROODING

Newly hatched young are not warm-blooded like their parents and must be brooded for several days until they can maintain their own body temperature. At night and during cool days, the parent will warm the nestlings by sitting in the incubation posture. On hot days, parents may stand over the young to provide shade.

Northern Cardinal

NEST CLEANING

To keep the nest safe from predators, many birds remove eggshells after hatching. Excrement from the young of most small land birds emerges in "portable" casings called fecal sacs. Parents usually remove the sacs as they emerge from the cloaca of the nestlings and either consume them or carry them away from the nest.

BEHAVIOR-WATCHING ACTIVITIES

Birders can provide useful contributions to ornithology while adding a new dimension to birding fun. Ethograms, time budgets, and behavior sequences are commonly used behavior-watching methods that will help to focus your attention on the many behaviors that birds perform during the day and how they budget their time between social interactions and body maintenance.

Building an Ethogram

Derived from ethology, the study of animal behavior, an ethogram is a precise catalog of all the behavior patterns of an animal. By carefully watching resident birds throughout the year, you can collect a list of behaviors for each species and assemble ethograms for local birds.

CHOOSE YOUR SUBJECT

Start by selecting one local breeding bird to observe. The behavioral repertoire of nonbreeding birds is not as great, as they are more difficult to keep under observation and to follow through the seasons.

CONDUCT PRELIMINARY RESEARCH

Consult the literature before starting your field observation (see appendix). Even with a search of ornithological journals, you may find few studies about your species because so much remains unknown.

TAKE NOTES

After reviewing the literature, take field notes, listing and describing the behaviors you see. In addition to the common behaviors, watch for behaviors and social displays that may be unique to your species.

NAME BEHAVIORS

If the behavior doesn't exist in the literature, give it a short descriptive term based on the most conspicuous action. Then describe the display in detail.

DESCRIBE BEHAVIOR

For each behavior include a detailed description of the actions within the behavior or display, followed by a separate discussion paragraph if you have an interpretation about the display.

BUILD AN ETHOGRAM

Build an ethogram by assembling a list of behaviors from your field notes. List behaviors under two major categories: body care (include feeding strategies) and social displays.

A courtship display of Great Blue Herons

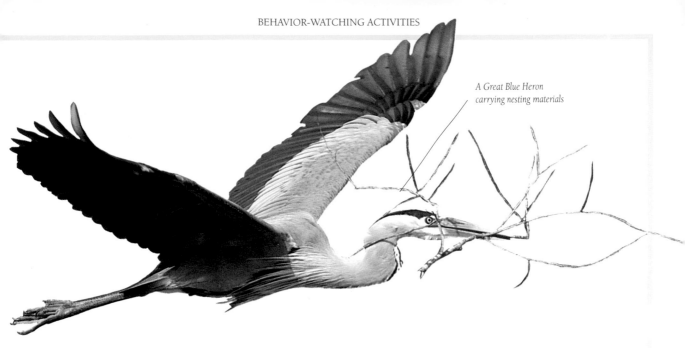

A Great Blue Heron carrying nesting materials

In the following descriptions of the behavior of the Great Blue Heron, note that displays consist of a predictable sequence of actions and that the name of the behavior is derived from the most conspicuous action in the display. Other Great Blue Heron courtship display names include Circle Flight, Crest Raising, Fluffed Neck, Bill Duel, Bill Clappering, and Stretch. Names for vocalizations, such as Landing Call and Aerial Call, indicate the predictable circumstance during which the vocalization is produced.

Twig Shake: The heron extends its neck slowly, grasps a branch in its mandibles, and shakes it side to side or forward and backward....

Arched Neck: Quickly the heron erects its plumes (crest, scapular, and basal portions of the neck) and curves its neck like a rainbow so that the closed bill usually points below horizontal. It maintains this position up to five seconds before relaxing to a standing posture.

Avoid adding interpretations about function to display names. Such adjectives may bias other observers from making independent observations. Names such as Aggressive Head Lowering or Distress Call suggest that the meaning of the behavior or vocalization is clearly known when, in fact, the circumstance and value of the display may be unknown or in dispute. If you have an idea about function, survival value, or origin of a display, include this in a brief statement under your description.

Twig Shake: The heron extends its neck slowly, grasps a branch in its mandibles, and shakes it side to side or forward and backward....

Discussion: The variability found in the Twig Shake's form may enable it to carry a large amount of "graded" information: Vigorous performances may well express redirected aggression. The Twig Shake presumably evolved from nest-building motor patterns, which it still resembles.

Identifying a Behavioral Sequence

Bird behavior usually follows a fairly predictable sequence of events depending on the season, time of year, and weather. This sequence becomes readily apparent if you concentrate on the activities of an individual bird. Select a bird that is attending a nest or a large waterbird that is likely to stay within your field of view for most of a three-hour period. Record the behaviors you see in the field-note format, then assign a behavior category to each observation.

House Sparrow

In a study of the House Sparrow, the following categories were assigned to the activities of a male House Sparrow that was busy attending its young.

A Agonistic Behaviors (threat and appeasement displays)
C Caution Behaviors (alert postures)
F Foraging (collecting food for self and nestling)
N Feeding Nestlings (entering and delivering food at the nest)
B Body-Care Behaviors (preening, bathing, dusting)

Publishing Your Observations

If you observe an unusual behavior or conduct a thorough behavioral study, discuss your observations with professionals at a local museum or university. Your observations may be worthy of publication. If, after checking these resources, you believe that your observations are unique, study appropriate formats and write a short note or paper for one of the bird journals described in the appendix.

Agonistic behavior of House Sparrows.

The behavioral sequence emerges by assigning a category to each observation in the field notes. Following is a sample of the sequence of behaviors performed by the male House Sparrow:

A (F C N) A (F C N) (F C N) B (F C N) (F C N) (F C N) B (F C N) B

The routine of this sparrow is apparent from the above sequence. This bird was clearly committed to the routine of foraging for food, cautiously approaching the nest, then feeding the young (FCN). This was interrupted only by threats to the nest from potential predators (A) and occasional preening and bathing (B).

Clocking a Time Budget

In addition to demonstrating predictable sequences in bird behavior, your field notes can also show how much time birds spend on each activity. To construct a time budget, simply total the time for all observations within each behavioral category. During three hours of observation, the male House Sparrow used his time as follows:

House Sparrow

Behavior Category	Time (minutes)	% of Total Time
Agonistic	32	18
Caution	40	22
Foraging	68	38
Feeding Nestlings	9	5
Body Care	31	17
	180	100

To represent the time budget on a pie chart, calculate angles by multiplying 360 degrees by the percentage of time for each behavior category. Draw a circle with a compass and measure angles with a protractor. Sketches of typical behaviors lend a nice touch (see chapter Four).

feeding young 5%

resting and preening 17%

agonistic 18%

caution 22%

foraging (also feeding himself) 38%

This pie chart illustrates the time budget of a male House Sparrow.

Tips for Behavior Watchers

Although behaviors may be similar for different individuals of the same species, there will also be variations arising from different personalities. It takes a keen field observer to recognize individual personalities, but this offers an additional challenge that gives behavior watching infinite appeal. Focus your observation with these points in mind:

- Record circumstances surrounding your observations. Include location, time of day, weather, and presence of other animals.
- Quantify observations by noting how long, how many times, or in what sequence behaviors occur.
- Consider your effect(s) on the behavior you are watching. Minimize your presence by using binoculars and by watching from a blind or other cover.
- Keep interpretations separate from descriptions, and avoid assigning human motives to behavior.
- Be patient, especially if you are watching during the "off hours," between 11 A.M. and 3 P.M., when birds are less active.

TAKING FIELD NOTES

A small investment of time taking notes in the field and later organizing them at home can produce a valuable set of field notes. Such notes will have increasing value if they can be clearly interpreted by others and if information is available for quick retrieval. The sections that follow offer suggestions for improving your note-taking skills and for filing observations for quick retrieval.

Checklists

Checklists are the most frequently used type of field record, but, unfortunately, most lists contribute little to our understanding of bird distributions and abundance. Most observers simply check off the species they have seen without indicating the number seen or providing details about where the birds were observed. In searching for new and unusual species, some birders ignore the most abundant birds. Such records would be much more valuable if they included an actual count or an estimate of numbers for all species.

In addition to indicating numbers, always note the exact location (direction in air miles from nearest town), hours in the field, and weather conditions. Most checklists provide space for these items. With these basics, your checklist will have meaning for future use. Information from a number of observers over a broad area can serve as an early warning signal that a formerly abundant species is experiencing a serious population decline.

Complete, personal, daily checklists are useful for preparing and updating local and regional checklists, and their value increases with time because such counts provide important baseline data for detecting population changes.

Field Notebooks

While in the field keep a pocket notebook for recording observations. When describing field marks and behaviors of unknown or unusual birds, include details of color, plumage, and behavior as well as observation conditions, such as lighting, approximate distance from the birds, and names of other people who saw the birds. To verify field observations, it is important to observe unknown birds systematically for field marks and behaviors. Note these at the time of observation, so that details are not forgotten.

Abbreviations

Whenever possible, use abbreviations, but be certain to include a key so that there is no doubt about the meaning of your notations. The following are a few standard abbreviations:

Sp. Acct. = Species Account
♂, ♂♂ = male, males
♀, ♀♀ = female, females
imm. = immature
N/C = nest under construction
N4E = nest with four eggs

N3Y = nest with 3 young
A/F = adult carrying food
HO = heard only
DOR. = dead on road
FO = flying over
~ = approximately (for example, ~100 = approx. 100)

Preserving Your Field Notes

It doesn't take long for serious field observers to collect a small mountain of notebooks filled with checklists, Species Accounts, and Journal entries. If the data are well prepared, they will become increasingly valuable and deserve protection. A duplicate copy of the notes or storage in a fireproof safe are important considerations. Do not underestimate the value of your field records. Your notes may be the necessary documentation for future restorations if the species you describe disappears from local habitats in the future.

Record the date and time, and location of observations

Note the names of any other people who saw the birds. Thorough written descriptions by several people will help verify unknown birds at a later time and are often accepted by authorities as the basis for legitimate sight records.

Assign names to specific behaviors and then describe the behaviors in detail.

With practice, a quick sketch can capture behaviors and map your descriptions of field marks. A good technique for recording field marks is to start by looking at the bird's head and work your way back to the tail.

FIELD IDENTIFICATION REPORT

Date: _____ Habitat: _____

Location: _____
(Distance from nearest city)

Weather: Temperature _____,
Wind _____, % Cloud Cover _____
(Direction/Speed)

Observers: Binoculars   Spotting Scope
(Circle One)

Distance from Bird:

Field Marks:

Behavior:

Vocalizations:

Comments (Sketch):

The Grinnell Field Note System

Established by Joseph Grinnell of the Museum of Vertebrate Zoology, University of California at Berkeley, this system is based on three record-keeping sections: the Catalog, the Species Accounts, and the Journal. Grinnell's Catalog is widely used by museum workers to list collected specimens with details about locality, measurements, and so on. His system of recording Species Accounts and Journal entries has a much broader application and is the standard tool of many field observers.

Grinnell insisted on recording field observations directly into Species Accounts and Journal notebooks while in the field to avoid loss of detail and errors resulting from transposing. However, a pocket field notebook or tape recorder provides a convenient way to record details under rigorous field conditions and while traveling.

Species Accounts

Soon after returning home from the field, transfer observations from your field notebook to individual Species Accounts. In this system, observations about a particular species are grouped together, either as lists or sightings, or as more detailed behavioral or identification accounts. The great benefit of the system is that all observations about a species are grouped together, rather than spread throughout your field notes or Journal. In this system, the Species Accounts appear on loose-leaf pages. The loose-leaf feature permits you to add additional pages to existing notes on each species. To keep your Species Accounts organized, arrange them to follow the taxonomic order presented on a field checklist. Add observations of special interest to a list of running accounts, giving date, exact locality, number of individuals, nests, eggs, and any details about age, sex, or behavior. Keep running accounts only for selected species that are of personal interest. The system is especially useful for recording unusual or declining species.

Northern Harrier

Journal

The Journal is a daily summary of your itinerary and observations, with supporting details about weather, names of field companions, and places visited. Most observers prefer loose-leaf notebooks, but bound Journals are also adequate. The Journal provides an excellent place to tally the species you've seen during the day by transferring lists and numbers from your field notebook, tape recorder, or checklist. Underline unusual species or numbers, and note which birds are detailed further in your Species Accounts notebook.

Northern Harrier

SAMPLE SPECIES ACCOUNT

Following the format of this sample page from a Species Account on the Northern Harrier, all sightings for a species should be listed on the same page. Additional loose-leaf pages can be added when necessary.

Organize detailed descriptions of unusual birds and behavioral notes in your Species Account notebook.

Species Accounts need not be limited to unusual birds. Pick a common bird that interests you and start assembling Species Accounts.

Localities should be underlined, and these names should correspond to Journal entries for the same date.

Detailed behavioral accounts should also be transferred from your field notebook to a page in your Species Accounts notebook.

The preferred paper size is approximately 8½ by nine inches.

When you see an unusual or unfamiliar bird, take abundant field notes, describing all details, and add this information to your Species Accounts. Also include comments about unusual events of the day, but do not enter detailed accounts; they are easily lost in your Journal entries and are easier to retrieve from your Species Accounts.

T. L. Fleischner
1999

Northern Harrier

2 April <u>Nisqually Delta, Thurston Co., Wash.</u>
1000: ♀ flying S approx. 3 m. above ground. Was being harassed by a common crow.

19 April <u>5 mi. N of Beatty, Nevada</u>
0800: ♂ flying on E side of US-95

20 April <u>Alvord Hot Springs, Harney Co., Oregon</u>
1300: ♂ flying low, hunting. Just N of hot springs.

21 April <u>Malheur N.W.R., Harney Co., Oregon</u>
1105: ♀ - comi. S of field station on Center Patrol Rd. Flying 2 m. off ground, having trouble flying into strong S wind.
1215: ♂ - 13.4 mi. S of field station on Center Patrol Rd.
1700: 3 flying together, 5.0 mi. E of junction Orc. 205 and road to Diamond Craters.

18 May: <u>near Migraine Lake Campground, Columbia NWR, Grant Co., Wash.</u>
0515: First saw ♂, then ♀, flying over marsh, coming within 10 ft of me. Flew in large circles around marsh, ♀ making distress call. Every time they were in the N part of their circular flight pattern, 20-30 red-winged blackbirds would fly up and harass them. They perched ~ 1 min. on 25m. high cliff, then circled out to E and dropped to ground. ♀ was missing one secondary on each wing. It appeared that they had a nest amongst the tall rushes there. We left at 0530, they were no longer visible.

Tips for Creating Journals and Species Accounts

For Species Accounts include your name, year, date, locality, and commentary. For Journal entries include all of the above plus route of travel, weather, habitat description, and species list. Record all information consecutively. Don't begin a new page for each new entry; each page should be capable of standing alone. Repeat your name, year, and date on each page, noting "continued," if an entry extends from one page to the next. Write concisely, avoid slang, and use standard abbreviations. Use the international 24-hour clock system to report times. Make time to compile Journal entries from your field notes at the end of each day. If you fall behind, do the current day before going back to catch up on previous days.

NOTE-TAKING EQUIPMENT

The proper choice of paper and ink will greatly enhance the life of notes and their legibility in years to come. Species Accounts and Journal entries are best recorded with a technical pen and a quick-drying, waterproof black ink. Select paper with a high rag content. It will hold the ink better and will not turn yellow and brittle with age.

COUNTING BIRDS

The ability to count birds accurately is a skill that comes only with considerable practice. It becomes increasingly difficult to make exact counts when birds occur in large numbers or where several species are present together. But even difficult, laborious counts are more useful than "ballpark estimates." The challenge is to give as accurate a count as possible.

Depending on such variations as lighting and distance, it is best to record round numbers when exact counts are not possible. A flock containing a hundred or fewer individuals should be rounded off to the nearest five to ten birds; a flock with more than a hundred birds may be rounded to the nearest twenty-five or fifty, depending on viewing opportunities. Avoid giving range estimates of birds, such as "approximately three hundred to five hundred," since such estimates are unnecessarily vague and are difficult to compare with other counts.

Counting Flocks

Flocks of flying birds, such as waterfowl, shorebirds, and blackbirds, are among the most difficult to count. Their speed, movement, and habit of flying in dense, three-dimensional flocks contribute to the difficulty of achieving reasonable estimates.

If you are attempting to determine the number of birds congregating at a certain point (such as herons or blackbirds returning to a roost), sample the number passing a fixed point (such as a tree or a house) in one-minute intervals throughout the period during which the birds return. Average your one-minute counts and multiply the average by sixty. Determine the total duration of the procession from start to finish, then multiply this time period (in minutes) by the number of birds seen in an average minute.

Blocking

Exact counts are usually possible if there are fewer than thirty birds in a flying flock. For larger numbers try a technique called blocking. This approach consists simply of counting a block of birds of typical density from the trailing end of the flock and then visually superimposing this block onto the rest of the flock to see how many times it will fit. For example, if a flock contains about sixty birds, your block need only contain the trailing twenty birds in the group, and this would "fit" onto the remainder of the flock two more times.

For huge flocks, start by estimating part of the group to represent a block of fifty to a hundred birds. Then use this sample to arrive at a total estimate, just as with smaller numbers. Concentrate on memorizing impressions of what different size flocks look like. With practice you can develop mental images because different groupings have distinctive shapes and forms.

The blocking technique permits estimates of large flocks. Count the number of birds in a sample block and then see how many additional times this block can be superimposed on the remainder of the flock.

PRACTICING BIRD COUNTS

Many North American bird censuses and surveys rely on amateur participants. The success of these studies depends largely on the counting skills of participants. Skill at estimating bird numbers depends largely on practice. A good way to sharpen estimating accuracy is to make a set of flash cards with different numbers of dots. Mark the number of dots on the back of the cards and then have a friend check your counting ability by flashing the cards at various moving speeds. A similar system consists of having a friend toss precounted samples of beans or popcorn onto a tabletop. Practice making quick estimates until you achieve accuracy within 5 percent.

You can also practice your estimating skill by making projection slides with different numbers of dots. Project the slides at a bird club meeting and compare estimates. Such slides are easily made by poking pinholes into two-by-two-inch pieces of cardboard or opaque color slides. Challenge club members by keeping the "flocks" on the screen for only a few seconds. This exercise is especially useful in training group members to participate in such counts as the Audubon Christmas Bird Count.

A

B

C

D

Practice the blocking technique of counting birds with these flock patterns. The number of birds in the illustrations can be found on the last page of the book.

SKETCHING BIRDS

Any careful observer can make useful field sketches. Regardless of artistic quality, field sketches serve as valuable visual records of the birds you encounter. Start by sketching in the field, and you'll be surprised at the additional details of form and behavior you begin to notice. Familiarize yourself with basic bird anatomy, noting the bends of the wing and leg and how these limbs attach to the avian skeleton. Look at the shape and posture of the body, paying special attention to the relative proportions of head, wings, and tail. Consider bird anatomy as you sketch, carefully noting positions of head, wings, tail, and legs.

Bird Skeleton Versus Human

Adaptations for flight have affected bird anatomy in many ways, but similarities to the human skeleton remain obvious.

Ostrich

Thigh bone (Femur)
Knee
Drumstick (Tibia and Fibula)
Ankle
Foot bones (Tarsus)
Toes (Phalanges)

Shoulder
Upper arm (Humerus)
Elbow
Forearm (Radius and Ulna)
Palm
Fingers (Phalanges)
Thumb
Fingers (Phalanges)
Elbow
Center of gravity
Wrist
Wrist
Shoulder
Elbow

Turkey Vulture

Note that the avian thigh bone (femur) is shortened and buried in the bird's body with the forward end lying near the bird's center of gravity. The drumstick bone (tibia and fibula) emerges from the bird's body ending in the ankle. Foot bones are fused into one bone called the tarsus, which points forward, ending back at the bird's center of gravity. Birds walk, hop, stand, and run on their toes.

Birds wings are attached above and slightly forward of the center of gravity. When a bird unfolds its wings over its back, the upper arm (humerus) points backward to the elbow, where it connects with the forearm (radius and ulna), which bends forward ending at the wrist. Elongated and fused hand bones point back toward the tail. Wing bones fold together compactly when the bird is at rest.

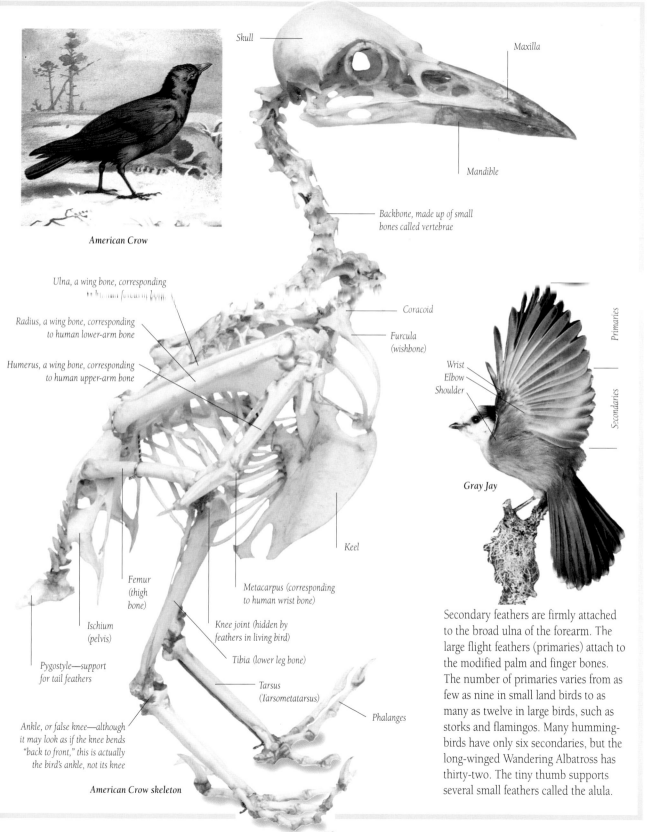

American Crow

Skull

Maxilla

Mandible

Backbone, made up of small
bones called vertebrae

Ulna, a wing bone, corresponding
to human forearm bone

Radius, a wing bone, corresponding
to human lower-arm bone

Humerus, a wing bone, corresponding
to human upper-arm bone

Coracoid

Furcula
(wishbone)

Wrist
Elbow
Shoulder

Primaries

Secondaries

Gray Jay

Keel

Femur
(thigh
bone)

Metacarpus (corresponding
to human wrist bone)

Ischium
(pelvis)

Knee joint (hidden by
feathers in living bird)

Tibia (lower leg bone)

Pygostyle—support
for tail feathers

Tarsus
(Tarsometatarsus)

Phalanges

Ankle, or false knee—although
it may look as if the knee bends
"back to front," this is actually
the bird's ankle, not its knee

American Crow skeleton

Secondary feathers are firmly attached
to the broad ulna of the forearm. The
large flight feathers (primaries) attach to
the modified palm and finger bones.
The number of primaries varies from as
few as nine in small land birds to as
many as twelve in large birds, such as
storks and flamingos. Many hummingbirds have only six secondaries, but the
long-winged Wandering Albatross has
thirty-two. The tiny thumb supports
several small feathers called the alula.

FLIGHT POSTURES

In these common flight postures—
soaring, upstroke, downstroke,
and landing—note the positions of
the wings and how birds variously
use the tail as a balance rudder or
brake to assist wing action.

Canada Goose

Wrist

Elbow

Shoulder

Willet

UPSTROKE

Under-tail coverts

Shoulder

Elbow

Wrist

SOARING

Broad Tail

Scapulars

Upper-tail coverts

Black-capped Chickadee

DOWNSTROKE

Wrist

Wrist

LANDING

Toes

Black-billed Magpie

Fanned tail

Standing

Walking

Magnolia Warbler

Perching

Sitting

These four illustrations show a perching bird leg in various
postures and the position of the toes and leg bones as the
bird stands, walks, perches, and sits.

Assembling a Field Sketch

Start your field sketch with an oval that approximates the general proportions of the bird. Whether you intend to sketch an owl, heron, or robin, they all have oval (egg-shaped) bodies. It is the differences in wings, tails, and legs that give each species a distinctive form. Watch carefully to see at what angle the bird holds its body, then begin to assemble body parts, outlining head and neck, wings, tail, and legs. Concern yourself with proportions of the different parts to one another and the position of attachment, always referring back to the living bird. Portray most behaviors by changing the posture of the bird's body (position of the oval) and the position of its appendages. If you see an unusual bird or one you can't identify, quickly draw a standard perching posture and then add details to illustrate distinctive field marks, carefully noting the position of its appendages.

Draw with smooth, flowing lines to achieve an outline sketch of the bird. Don't bother to erase mistakes. The goal is to capture shape and posture with as few lines as possible before the bird flies away. Practice by sketching tame birds, such as captive parakeets, pigeons, or feeder birds. Sitting postures are easiest, but it won't take long before a few pencil lines will also capture the movement of birds in flight.

Sketch birds in your field notebook or in a small artist's spiral sketchbook using a soft HB pencil, adding finer details with a harder pencil, such as a 4H. An art gum eraser is useful for cleaning up sketches, but erasures should be kept to a minimum. After returning home, transfer sketches to your Species Accounts notebook or Journal.

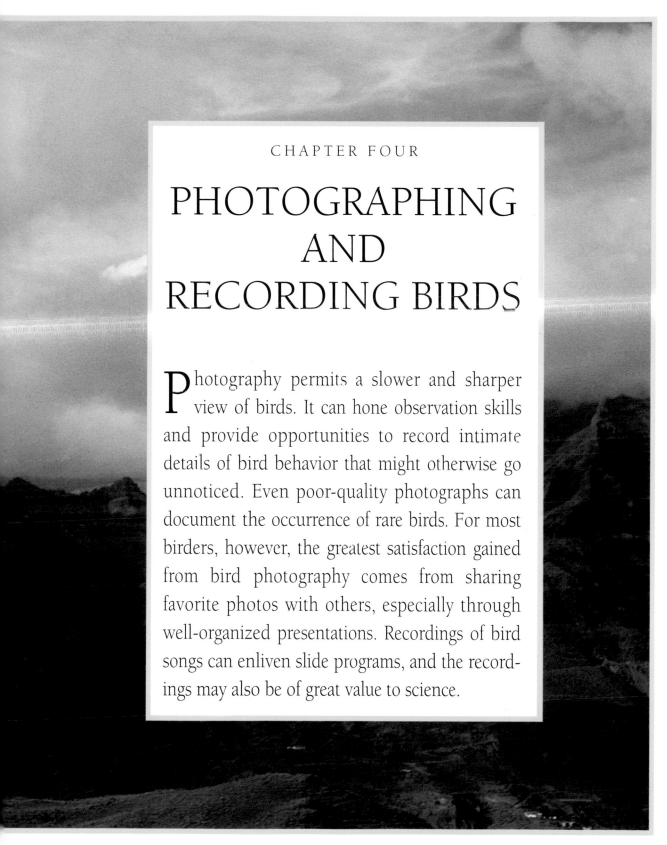

CHAPTER FOUR

PHOTOGRAPHING AND RECORDING BIRDS

Photography permits a slower and sharper view of birds. It can hone observation skills and provide opportunities to record intimate details of bird behavior that might otherwise go unnoticed. Even poor-quality photographs can document the occurrence of rare birds. For most birders, however, the greatest satisfaction gained from bird photography comes from sharing favorite photos with others, especially through well-organized presentations. Recordings of bird songs can enliven slide programs, and the recordings may also be of great value to science.

SINGLE-LENS REFLEX CAMERAS

Most bird photographers prefer the 35 mm single-lens reflex (SLR) format. Because 35 mm cameras are lightweight and compact, they are ideal for birders already encumbered with binoculars and field guides. SLR cameras have interchangeable lenses, offering the flexibility to photograph both close-ups and telephoto views.

Diverse opinions about the various merits of different models and the comparative value of various features can make selection of the "right" camera a bewildering experience. Do not let such debates get in the way of selecting a camera. Any of the better 35 mm SLR models are suitable for bird photographs.

Even with an automatic camera, it takes an experienced and sensitive photographer to spot an opportunity, compose the picture, consider the light, and snap the shutter before the bird disappears from the field of view.

SLR camera with 400 mm telephoto lens

Telephoto lenses

The magnifying power of a telephoto lens is indicated by the focal length of the lens. Magnification increases by one power for every 50 mm increase in focal length. For example, a 100 mm telephoto lens makes the subject look twice as close as it would through a standard (normal) 50 mm lens. Likewise, a 400 mm telephoto would magnify a subject eight times and be equivalent to an 8x binocular.

Tripods

It is difficult to hold a long telephoto lens steady—especially if you are attempting to photograph birds from a rocking boat. Usually it is inadvisable to hold a telephoto larger than 300 mm by hand. Steady such telephotos with a sturdy tripod or other support. One exception to the 300 mm rule are lenses with built-in image stabilization, which allows holding long lenses by hand at slower than normal shutter speeds.

To fill the camera field of view, it is important to be able to focus at close distances to the subject. Close-focusing capability is especially useful for small birds—even with a 400 mm lens one must approach surprisingly close to take an interesting picture. For birds the size of this warbler, the lens must focus to approximately fifteen feet to fill the field.

Blackpoll Warbler

Aperture sizes

Shutter release button

Shutter and film speed dial

Flash hot shoe

Film rewind knob

Ring for strap attachment

Aperture scale

Distance scale

A typical 35 mm camera

Interchangeable lenses offer great flexibility

f2—1/60 sec

f2.8—1/30 sec

f4—1/15 sec

f5.6—1/8 sec

f8—1/4 sec

f11—1/2 sec

f16—1 sec

The speed of the lens refers to the maximum diaphragm opening (aperture) available. Aperture size is expressed as f numbers; the smaller the f number, the larger the aperture opening. Telephoto lenses with larger maximum apertures permit the use of faster shutter speeds, which reduces vibrations and results in sharper pictures. For example, a lens with a maximum aperture of f/8 might permit shooting at 1/125 second, but a lens with a maximum aperture of f/5.6 would, under the same conditions, permit shooting at 1/250 second and result in a sharper picture. Fast lenses also brighten viewing fields, which makes it easier to focus accurately and quickly. However, fast lenses have correspondingly wider diameter objective lenses, and the additional glass makes them both heavier and more expensive. Within limits, these are generally worthwhile trade-offs for the sharper pictures that result. For these reasons, it is best to avoid telephotos that are slower than f5.6.

SHUTTER SPEEDS

Large telephoto lenses require fast shutter speeds to reduce vibrations and the chance of blurred images. Using a medium-speed film (such as ISO 100), a shutter speed of 1/60 second is usually adequate for lenses with focal length of 100mm or less. Longer telephotos require faster shutter speeds. For comparison, the minimum shutter speed for lenses in the 100–300 mm range should be 1/250 second. If light permits, larger lenses require even faster shutter speeds. However, if an unusual bird appears or an interesting behavior occurs, it is well worth the cost of film to brace your lens, hold your breath, and take a chance at a slower shutter speed. With practice and a critical review of processed photos, you will soon learn how steady you can hold your various lenses.

Wandering Albatross

All-glass Versus Mirror Telephotos

There are two basic telephoto lens designs: all-glass and mirror. All-glass telephoto lenses offer the sharpest images, brightest fields of view, and best color rendition. Their principal drawbacks are bulky size and heavy weight, which make them difficult to carry in the field and hold steady. Mirror lenses are comparatively easy to carry in the field because of their lighter weight and compact design. They also offer a better close-focusing capability than most all-glass telephotos.

However, the mirror design may produce color shift, light falloff at the border of the picture, and donut-shaped patterns in the background. Another drawback is the slow, fixed aperture (usually f/8), which makes mirror lenses harder to focus and difficult to use in low-light situations. All-glass lenses are the usual choice of professional bird photographers.

Mirror telephoto lens

All-glass telephoto lens

Depth of Field

Telephoto lenses usually produce photos with a characteristically shallow depth of field (the depth of the picture that is in focus). Depth of field decreases as magnification (focal length) and aperture size increase. Depth is further reduced by focusing on close subjects. For example, a 400 mm lens opened to f/5.6 and focused at fifteen feet has a depth of field of only one inch!

To increase the amount of depth in your pictures, "stop down" the lens diaphragm to a smaller opening (larger f number), but remember that this means shooting at a slower shutter speed and risking blurred pictures from too much movement.

AUTOMATIC VERSUS PRESET LENSES

If you choose an all-glass telephoto, you must then select either an automatic or a preset design. The diaphragm of an automatic lens can be set at the preferred opening, but it will not actually close down until the shutter is released. This permits focusing with the lens wide open, a feature that facilitates sharper and quicker focusing. In contrast, preset lenses are slower to use because the lens diaphragm must be closed manually to a preselected opening after focusing with the diaphragm wide open. Focusing considerations are especially important for bird photography, because telephoto lenses have a shallow depth of field, and the active nature of birds usually necessitates frequent focusing adjustments.

AUTOFOCUS LENSES

For photographing birds in flight, autofocus telephotos in the range of 300 mm permit you to follow a flying bird and shoot multiple sequences as the bird moves. The autofocus feature can be disabled for other uses where it is not helpful or may be a hindrance. Autofocus can be annoying because the lens is constantly focusing on whatever is in the center of the field of view, while often you may want the subject off center.

ZOOM LENSES

Lenses with zoom focal-length combinations such as 70–210 mm and 100–300 mm offer a convenient way to photograph birds at varying distances with a minimum amount of lens juggling. Macro zooms offer added convenience by doubling as a close-up lens, permitting the photographer to focus on everything from the distant horizon to subjects within a few inches of the lens. However, beware of the lower-priced zoom lenses, because they are likely to produce less-than-crisp images and may suffer from loss of light at the edges of the field.

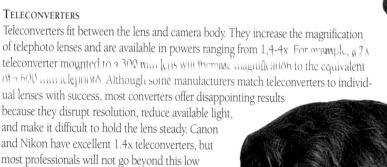

Zoom lens

Teleconverter

TELECONVERTERS

Teleconverters fit between the lens and camera body. They increase the magnification of telephoto lenses and are available in powers ranging from 1.4-4x. For example, a 2 x teleconverter mounted to a 300 mm lens will increase magnification to the equivalent of a 600 mm telephoto. Although some manufacturers match teleconverters to individual lenses with success, most converters offer disappointing results because they disrupt resolution, reduce available light, and make it difficult to hold the lens steady. Canon and Nikon have excellent 1.4x teleconverters, but most professionals will not go beyond this low magnification because of excessive loss of light.

Hand supports weight of telephoto lens

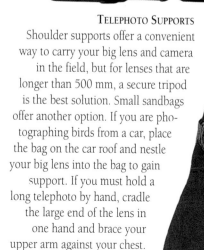

TELEPHOTO SUPPORTS

Shoulder supports offer a convenient way to carry your big lens and camera in the field, but for lenses that are longer than 500 mm, a secure tripod is the best solution. Small sandbags offer another option. If you are photographing birds from a car, place the bag on the car roof and nestle your big lens into the bag to gain support. If you must hold a long telephoto by hand, cradle the large end of the lens in one hand and brace your upper arm against your chest.

Flash Equipment

Electronic flash equipment can make it possible to photograph birds on overcast days and to adequately light such dark habitats as forests and thickets. Flash equipment is most useful for moderately close-up work, such as photographing birds at nests and feeders.

Features to consider when selecting a flash unit are brightness, duration of flash, the time it takes between exposures for the light to become ready for reuse (recycling interval), and the bulk and weight of the unit. Flash units are rated for brightness by their guide numbers; the larger the guide number, the brighter the flash. The duration of the flash should be at least 1/1000 second to stop bird movements. When selecting an electronic flash, it's best to obtain a through-the-lens (ttl) metering system which automatically determines the amount of light produced by the flash.

Great Horned Owls

Nocturnal animals are rarely seen in daylight. If you wish to photograph them you need to shoot them at night with flash equipment.

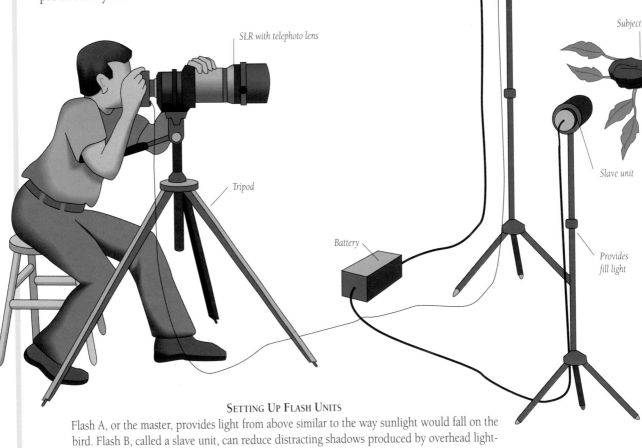

SLR with telephoto lens

Master flash unit

Subject

Slave unit

Tripod

Battery

Provides fill light

SETTING UP FLASH UNITS

Flash A, or the master, provides light from above similar to the way sunlight would fall on the bird. Flash B, called a slave unit, can reduce distracting shadows produced by overhead lighting. Slave units are cordless light sources synchronized to flash simultaneously with the master flash. Mount the slave unit on a tripod and direct the light at the bird's perch from the front and to the side to provide fill light that washes out shadows from the master flash.

Flash Units

An inexpensive flash with a guide number of approximately 65 is adequate for photographing birds within about three feet of the flash unit. To photograph birds at a nest or feeder, mount the flash unit on a tripod and position it approximately three feet from where the birds are likely to perch. Set your camera shutter to the special "x" synchronization speed, and calculate your aperture setting by dividing the flash unit's guide number by the distance to the subject (with experience you'll arrive at correction adjustments for your particular equipment).

Manual flash systems are adequate for nest and feeder photography; the flash is mounted on a tripod, and the distance to the bird is predictable. Shoot a test roll to establish the correct settings with your flash set at carefully measured distances from the subject. Don't trust the dial on the back of your flash unit. Once established, the f number will always be the same, and you won't have to worry about proper exposure. Then you'll be ready to capture the action when you see it.

Special automatic flash units designed to produce concentrated light for use with telephoto lenses are useful for stalking a bird where distance is not known and speed is critical. However, always take care that automatic units are not fooled by unusual lighting situations. If you suspect that your light unit may be fooled by backlighting, a white bird, or some other unusual situation, bracket the predicted f setting by also exposing frames at one-half and one full stop below and above to improve your chances of obtaining a satisfying photo.

Allen's Hummingbird

Flashes with durations of 1/15,000 second are necessary to stop the wings of hummingbirds.

FLASH EXTENDER
Increases flash output and enables photographers to shoot at greater distances with smaller apertures.

Flash

Flash extender

Telephoto lens

FILM AND PROCESSING

Color films are available either as transparency (slide) film or color print film. Most bird photographers prefer color slide film because it is less expensive per frame and because publishers prefer slides to color prints. A further advantage to using slide film is that while both color and black-and-white prints are easily made from transparencies, it is much more expensive to make slides from prints, and the results are less satisfying.

Different brands of 35 mm film

Types of Film

Regardless of manufacturer, slide films are easily recognized by the word "chrome" incorporated into the film name, e.g., Kodachrome, Agfachrome, and Fujichrome. Color print film names end with "color," e.g., Kodacolor and Agfacolor. Each type of color film has a somewhat different color emphasis, which is why certain daylight films, such as Kodachromes, emphasize warm colors such as browns and reds, while Ektachromes emphasize blue tones. For many years, Kodachrome was the standard for professional photographers, but new films with exceptionally rich, intense color are now available. Fujichrome films, such as Velvia, Sensia, and Provia, have become popular alternatives.

For the best reproduction quality, choose a film with a low "ISO" (formerly ASA) number. ISO is a measure of film speed (light sensitivity). While faster film speeds permit photography in darker situations, they do so only by compromising color and sharpness.

Processing

Before sending your film to a processor, consider that the quality of processing varies from one company to the next and that bargain processing offers are likely to produce inferior results. If you've invested in quality equipment and taken great care in the field to take the best photos possible, avoid sending film off for anything less than the best developing and printing processes.

Overexposed

Saturation

If your slides tend to be overexposed, try shooting with a smaller aperture (higher f stop number). This technique, called saturating the film, helps to avoid washed-out overexposures and results in richer colors and more detail. To saturate slide film in a camera with a manual light meter, simply select a lower f number (or faster shutter speed). This technique is just the opposite for color print films: to saturate color film, increase the aperture size. Automatic cameras are easily "fooled" into underexposing by a full stop by doubling the ISO setting. Experiment with the saturation technique by alternately shooting the same scene at normal and various saturated exposures.

Underexposed

Best   ***Chipping Sparrow***

BLACK-AND-WHITE PHOTOGRAPHY

While it might seem curious to consider taking black-and-white pictures of colorful birds, there is a timeless quality to black-and-white film. The appeal lies in the flexibility of the medium and the creative process, which can range from shooting photographs to developing and printing enlargements at home.

Eastern Kingbird

PHOTOGRAPHIC PROBLEMS

When photographs return from the processor, carefully sort them into two piles—one for those to keep, the other for discards. It's as important to study mistakes as it is to admire successes. Here are a few examples of common bird photography problems and some suggestions for increasing your number of "keepers."

SPECtacular Photos

Small subject size is the most common problem in bird photography because birds usually do their best to keep a safe distance between themselves and the photographer. The result is that birds often resemble a disappointing "speck" lost in excessive background. Learn the limits of your equipment, picturing in your mind what photos will look like when they return from the processor. Before tripping the shutter, take a moment to carefully examine the entire viewfinder of your single-lens reflex camera. It will show the exact contents of the future photograph—a cost-effective way to avoid taking SPECtacular pictures.

Vesper Sparrow

Angle of View

Too often, nature photographers tower over their diminutive subjects, resulting in uninteresting angles of view. Bird nests dramatically illustrate this problem. When a ground nest or shrub nest is discovered, the chicks flatten into the base of the nest to avoid detection. A view from the top, looking down, doesn't do justice to the nestlings, nest, or interaction with the parents. To capture the action in the nest, set up a photo blind positioned at eye level to the nest. Then, when one of the parents returns, you will have a better chance of capturing the drama of the food transfer. This approach takes enormous dedication of time and patience, but the result is worth the effort.

American Woodcock

"Soft" Images

There are two usual reasons for blurred or "soft" images. Either the subject moves out of the shallow depth-of-field focus, or the photo is taken at a shutter speed too slow to stop any movement. To identify pictures blurred from a focus problem, look for something either in front of or behind the bird that is in focus. This results from shooting at too slow a shutter speed. Autofocus lenses offer the best way to "stop" flying birds, but with skill, you can learn to follow and then "shoot" birds with a hand-held or shoulder-mounted telephoto. Usually it's necessary to set your shutter speed to at least 1/500 second, follow, focus, fire, and then shoot again. If birds are flying toward you, preset the focus at a known distance and wait for a bird to fly into the prefocused zone.

Common Grackle

Red-winged Blackbird nest

DISTRACTING BACKGROUNDS

While looking through the camera viewfinder, examine the background to see that it doesn't distract from or compete with the subject. Reduce background clutter by either filling the field of view with the subject, by moving the subject against a neutral background such as sky, or by reducing the depth of field (lower f number) to put background out of focus. Sometimes background can be improved by turning the camera from horizontal to vertical. Also, consider horizons when composing backgrounds. Slanting horizons have ruined more than a few otherwise impressive photos of birds flying over water; they result from too much concentration on the subject without adequate attention to background detail.

OVEREXPOSURES AND UNDEREXPOSURES

Extremely light or dark subjects can fool your camera's light meter and result in disappointing exposures. White-plumaged birds such as swans and gannets reflect more light than darker backgrounds in the same field of view. If your light meter reads the darker tones, the result will be washed-out subjects with poor color and lack of detail. Similarly, dark birds do not reflect as much light as the surrounding field, which frequently leads to underexposures. When possible, avoid these problems by first taking your exposure reading from a "neutral" surface, such as a medium gray or brown color near the subject. To properly expose white birds such as swans, gulls, and egrets, stop your diaphragm down by approximately one full f stop. Likewise, open your lens diaphragm to properly expose dark birds such as crows and blackbirds. Bracketing (shooting on either side of the recommended exposure) further guarantees at least a few properly exposed photos.

Mute Swan

LIGHTING PROBLEMS

Although backlighting can sometimes produce dramatic photographic effects, it is usually best to light subjects with direct lighting—unfortunately it is not always simple to arrange for sunlight to fall conveniently over your shoulder onto the subject. Flash equipment may provide adequate direct light on overcast days or in situations where a bird seldom leaves the shadows; flash units must be set within several feet of the subject or they will usually not cast enough light. But the most satisfying solution is simply to wait for direct light to fall where it is needed. Unless a bird nest is hidden under a porch or roof, it is usually possible to wait until the next clear morning or afternoon when the sun is in a more "cooperative" position.

Also consider the quality of available light. When possible, avoid exposing color film during the heat of the day when the sun is directly overhead (approximately from 11 A.M. to 2 P.M.). Such light is likely to produce harsh contrasts with disturbing glare from light-colored surfaces. Morning or late afternoon light contains warmer tones and will contribute more vital colors.

Pileated Woodpecker

BIRD BLINDS

Most birds quickly forget observers who hide within the cover of a bird blind. Nearly anything that hides the human form can function as a blind. Watch birds from a window of your home, a car, canoe, horseback, or from under a loose-fitting poncho, and you will find that birds will approach much closer than they would otherwise. Photographers can use this fact to great advantage by waiting in a blind at places that are likely to attract birds. A blind positioned near the nest of backyard birds will provide intimate views and excellent photographic opportunities.

Portable Blinds

Note the direction of the available light and background to determine the best location for a portable blind. Ideally, sunlight should fall directly onto the location where you expect to focus, and the background should not contain distractions, such as houses, telephone lines, or even "busy" vegetation.

Photographers must take special care when photographing active bird nests. To reduce the chance of nest desertion or predation it is best to wait until the young hatch before positioning the blind. First, set the blind approximately 20 feet from the nest for several days to give the birds a chance to accept this new feature to their landscape. Then, pick up the blind and set it closer, taking care to position it at eye level to the nest. Make certain that your blind can be assembled away from the nest and carried in one piece.

To permit a clear view of the young, it may be necessary to part the vegetation in front of the nest. Rather than cut a clear path and later expose nestlings to weather and predators, use string or masking tape to hold branches and leaves out of the way. Be certain to carefully return all cover to its original position over the nest at the close of each photographic session.

Common Redpoll

Birds usually have predictable ways of approaching nests and feeders. To obtain bird photos with natural settings, watch for approach routes and prefocus on a branch or other favorite perch. If birds are not perching in a suitable place for photos, position a convenience perch, such as a bare branch, to the feeder. Birds are usually quick to frequent such perches, giving the photograph a more natural look.

Designs for Building a Portable Bird Blind

Portable bird blinds should be no larger than necessary to provide shelter for a seated photographer and a minimum of equipment. Usually, three feet square is ample space. The frame should have a minimum of parts and be quick to assemble. Blinds that can be picked up and moved without disassembling permit the photographer to set a blind near a nest with a minimum of disturbance.

Burlap is an ideal material for covering the blind. Its wide weave keeps the blind from overheating and permits the photographer to observe birds approaching from any direction. Some birds, however, can detect movement through burlap, particularly if the blind is backlit. Canvas and camouflage nylon cloth are also popular blind covers. Regardless of material, the blind should have a snug-fitting cover that does not flap in the wind.

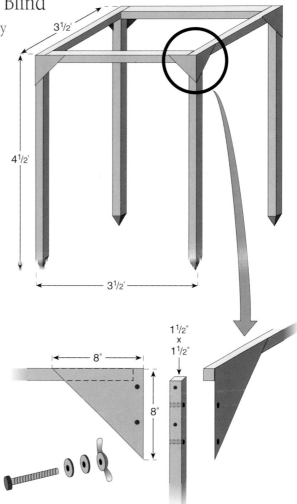

Build Your Own Blind

Construct this wooden-frame blind from eight sections of 1½-inch-square lumber. Permanently fix triangle braces to each end of the top, and join the corners by placing 1¾-inch stove bolts through the braces and uprights.

A window of your home might be the best bird blind for photographing backyard feeder birds. Place a bird feeder near a window, and it won't take long before the birds lose their shyness about your telephoto lens and approach to within easy photographic distance. Ideally, extend the lens through an open window, but if this is not possible, focus through the (cleaned) glass. Bold feeder birds such as chickadees and tit-mice will readily approach feeders with the photographer standing in full view at the window, but more timid subjects may only approach if the photographer hides from view.

FILING BIRD SLIDES

Aside from photographs of rare species or slides documenting unusual sightings or behaviors, the only slides worth keeping are those you would proudly show friends. If every "record shot" is kept, it soon become increasingly difficult to find your best slides, and if slides aren't easily found when you want them, what's the point of taking pictures?

Selection of an appropriate filing system depends on the number and variety of slides in your collection and the amount of time available for cataloging. Keep your system simple so that it doesn't become a chore to catalog and file the slides. Start by discarding rejects, and make it a high priority to file slides as soon as they return from the processor.

Examining Slides

10x loupe

When slides return from the processor, critically examine each slide by spreading them on a light table. Pull your best slides from the group and carefully examine the remainder to identify mistakes. To check for sharpness, examine the slides with a 10x loupe or hand lens. Then, before the rejects revive too many fond memories, toss them into the wastebasket or store them on a letter spike. The rationale of "I paid for it—why not keep it?" will lead to boring slide shows and a hopeless backlog of uncataloged slides. The first step in setting up a slide filing system is to mercilessly discard as many slides as possible.

A light table is essential for evaluating slides and organizing slide presentations. Commercially built light tables or "previewing screens" like this one are available at most camera shops. Or you can construct your own light table by building a box, painting the interior white or silver, and mounting fluorescent fixtures in a parallel circuit. Cover the box with a piece of white, opaque Plexiglas to complete the table.

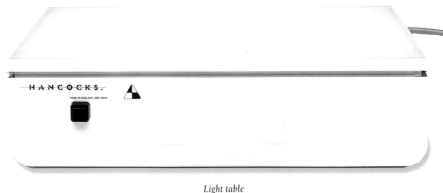

Light table

Organizing Slides

If you are already behind in filing slides or have yet to start, try this straightforward system, which makes slides easy to retrieve and also teaches the organization of bird orders and families.

The order and family names serve as an excellent structure for coding slides (see the appendix for a current listing of North American bird taxonomy). With this in mind, assign each order a distinct two-letter code and use this as the prefix in your coding system.

For example, all photos of Atlantic Puffins would receive the prefix CH for the order Charadriiformes and AL for Alcidae. If the first photograph you take of an alcid is an Atlantic Puffin, all future Atlantic Puffins would receive the alphanumeric code CH-AL-1. Place the code in the upper right hand corner of the slide, and record additional data, such as date and location, on the slide mount. File all CH-AL-1's together; to retrieve a particular Atlantic Puffin photo, you need simply pull all of the CH-AL-1 slides and spread them on your light table.

Five years might pass before you photograph another auk, such as the Common Murre. This second alcid receives the CH-AL-2 designation, and all future slides of Common Murres receive the same designation. Use plastic notebook sleeves (made from archival-quality plastic) or store slides in trays especially designed for the purpose.

Atlantic Puffin

Common Murre

Depending on the size of your slide collection, store the slides in small dust-tight slide filing boxes or in large cabinets like this one designed for this purpose. Small filing boxes are available at most camera shops. Avoid designs that have individual spaces for each slide, since they hold relatively few slides. Cardboard spacers labeled with the various orders and family codes will organize the slides within the boxes.

PRESENTING A SLIDE PROGRAM

One need not be a professional speaker to excite an audience with everyday adventures watching and photographing birds. Almost anyone who makes the effort to photograph birds can step in front of a group and win new friends for birds.

Bird clubs provide the most sympathetic audiences, but you should also attempt to reach people who have not yet discovered the satisfactions of watching birds. Garden clubs, hunting and fishing groups, and camera clubs are likely audiences. Most senior-citizens groups, scout organizations, and school classes will enthusiastically welcome visiting speakers. If your local bird club or Audubon chapter does not have its own speaker's bureau, consider organizing one.

It takes more than good slides to make an enjoyable, informative presentation. Here are some tips:

Planning Your Slide Presentation

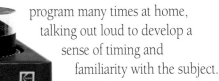

Slide projector

- Research your subject. Build your presentation around a theme, a specific habitat, or group of animals. Usually, in-depth, focused approaches work best, such as "Behaviors of Feeder Birds" or "Winter in the Deciduous Forest."
- Arrange to have someone stay with the projector to adjust focus and remove jammed slides. Also arrange for someone to turn off the room lights and bring them up again after your presentation. Use a remote projector advancer so that you can stand in front of the audience rather than behind the projector.
- Confidence in speaking, as well as the flow of your "patter," come only with practice. Review the program many times at home, talking out loud to develop a sense of timing and familiarity with the subject.
- Slide presentations for children should contain no more than seventy slides and should not last more than thirty minutes. Always provide an opportunity for children to ask questions.
- Maps are a must for slide programs dealing with locations. To avoid walking to the screen and searching for a particular locale, cut out an arrow and lay it in position, then photograph the map with a close-up lens.

Setting Up Your Presentation

- Set up your equipment and prefocus the first slide before the audience arrives. Run through the slides to make sure they are not upside down or backward.

- Place a two-by-two-inch cardboard square into the slide carrier of a carousel slide projector. This permits you to turn the projector on before starting and then to advance from the "blank" slide to your first picture. If you have less than a full tray, put a blank slide into the last slot of the tray to darken the screen. Never stun your audience by advancing to a glaring, white screen.
- Always use a public-address system in an auditorium or large room. Check out the system ahead of time to adjust the volume.
- Every slide in the tray should illustrate some point in your narration. Preview your presentation with this in mind and eliminate pictures if they do not fit into the theme of the presentation.

During Your Presentation

- Keep your presentations lively, interjecting amusing incidents, but don't strain to be funny. If something funny did happen, talk about it if it seems appropriate, but don't feel you must start with a funny introduction. Avoid getting a cheap laugh by making fun of the way an animal looks.
- Give a brief introduction before darkening the room. Tell the audience what you will talk about, but don't provide details in the introduction.
- Focus your eyes on different spots in the audience, rather than staring at the screen or your notes. Vary the loudness and pitch of your voice.
- Rather than explain what a slide illustrates, let the slide illustrate what you say. For example, when narrating a picture of a bluebird at a nest box, don't say, "You can see that bluebirds nest in homemade boxes." Instead say, "Bluebirds nest in homemade boxes." This avoids interpreting the slides and sticks to interpreting the birds.

- Your slides will serve as adequate lecture notes, if you've practiced. If necessary, put prepared notes on large note cards, but never read your presentation.
- Most slides should stay on the screen no more than fifteen seconds, but it is important to vary the pace. Presentations for adults using one projector should contain no more than eighty slides and should not last beyond one hour.
- Do not worry about minor mistakes. If a slide doesn't drop into place or the projector somehow skips a slide, keep the narration going rather than taking the time to fumble with the projector. Never back up to a slide that is already past, and never apologize—the audience will likely not even notice mistakes unless you point them out.
- End the presentation with a brief review of major points. The conclusion is the most important part of the program; it sets the final tone and provides the opportunity to send the audience off with your most important message.

Slide tray

RECORDING BIRD SOUNDS

If you succeed in capturing good bird sounds on tape and note field data while making the recordings, the recordings could make a valuable addition to a collection of bird vocalizations such as the one archived at Cornell University's Library of Natural Sounds. The songs and calls of even the most common birds are poorly known, and sound libraries welcome recordings to add to their collections.

You can also enliven your slide programs by including a few recorded bird sounds. During presentations, keep a tape recorder conveniently positioned to provide an occasional burst of typical sound. While the audience views a particular bird or habitat, sounds will make the performance more interesting and bring your audience measurably closer to sharing the feeling of your field experience.

Types of Recorders

To record bird sounds in the field, tape recorders must be battery powered and lightweight. Presently four formats are available: cassette, reel-to-reel, rotary digital audio tape (R-DAT), and MiniDisc. There are many manufacturers and models of recorders, microphones, and accessories available for recording birds. Because the choices change regularly and improvements are continuously appearing, recommendations of specific equipment are beyond the scope of this chapter. For a review of recommended recording equipment for birders, see the Cornell Laboratory of Ornithology home page (birds.cornell.edu).

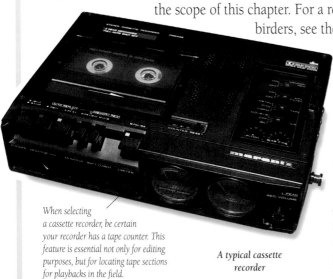

When selecting a cassette recorder, be certain your recorder has a tape counter. This feature is essential not only for editing purposes, but for locating tape sections for playbacks in the field.

A typical cassette recorder

CASSETTE RECORDERS

Most cassette models are lightweight and convenient to use in the field with a price significantly lower than other kinds of recorders. Top-quality cassette recorders cost $1,000 or more. Those priced around $300 can produce good fidelity recordings to accompany slide presentations, but they may not have the quality necessary to make consistently professional recordings. The principal drawback to the cassette recorder is the inconvenience of editing field tapes. Unlike the reel-to-reel design where the tape is easily cut and spliced, the tape on a cassette is hidden within the plastic cartridge. To edit a tape for a program using the cassette system, copy selected sections from field recordings onto a second recorder.

A reel-to-reel recorder's bulky size and hefty price tag make it impractical for most amateurs.

A typical reel-to-reel recorder

California Gull

REEL-TO-REEL RECORDERS

Field recordings made with a reel-to-reel recorder are easier to edit, and selected cuts can be spliced together to produce one tape with a composite of animal sounds. However, portable reel-to-reel recorders are much more expensive. The Swiss-made Nagra costs about $14,000, while a used machine is $2,000. Although reel-to-reel machines are more likely to produce recordings of professional quality with less background noise and a greater frequency range, they are also heavier and bulkier than cassette equipment.

DIGITAL RECORDERS

Digital audio recording is a new technology with great promise for recording bird songs. There are two popular types of digital recorders: rotary digital audio tape (R-DAT) and MiniDisc. Digital recorders convert sounds to a binary code stored either on magnetic tape or optical disc. R-DAT digital recorders record signals on magnetic tape; the MiniDisc format uses an optical disc for storage.

Digital machines are lightweight, typically weighing just two to four pounds, compared to the more than twenty pounds for a reel-to-reel machine. They are small, with dimensions similar to most cassette recorders. R-DAT cassettes have a maximum running time of two hours, and many units feature a convenient track indexing system that permits programming up to 99 randomly accessible points, a feature that allows future quick reference to specific recordings.

While a good cassette recorder will cost about $300 to $700, a comparable range for R-DAT recorders is $700 to $1,100. Two-head R-DAT and MiniDisc recorders have several serious drawbacks. These are: susceptibility to humidity, heavy power consumption, and inability for the recordist to listen to a recording while it is being made (even headphone monitoring is not adequate to determine if you are actually obtaining a recording). A more expensive, four-head R-DAT recorder will allow the recordist to monitor recordings while they are being made.

DAT tape

Promising new technology, DAT tapes and their recorders are small and lightweight.

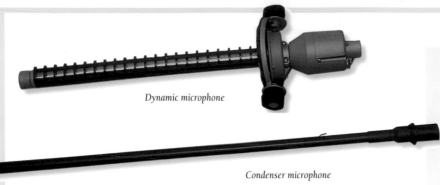

Dynamic microphone

Condenser microphone

Match the Microphone to the Recorder

Without a quality microphone, even a high-priced recorder will produce disappointing results; yet it is foolish to purchase a very expensive microphone for an inexpensive recorder. Make certain the microphone matches the recorder by checking to see that the impedance rating for the microphone is similar to the manufacturer's specifications for the recorder input.

Microphones

There are two basic types of microphones—dynamic and condenser. Dynamic microphones are often preferred for fieldwork because they are rugged and operate without an auxiliary power source. Condenser microphones produce recordings with high-quality sound and a wider frequency range, but their additional circuitry and auxiliary power supply may cause additional maintenance problems. For most bird song recordings, moderate priced microphones of either type will suffice.

When selecting a microphone, consider frequency range and sensitivity. To record most bird sounds, microphones should have a frequency range of between 50 and 15,000 hertz. To avoid tapes with hissing background sounds, avoid low-sensitivity microphones. Sensitivity is usually expressed in millivolts; the higher this figure, the greater the sensitivity. Manufacturers of high-quality microphones typically provide specifications that include frequency response and sensitivity.

A foam windscreen cover placed over the microphone reduces background noise.

Analogous to using a magnifying lens to focus light, a parabolic reflector captures sound waves by concentrating them to a single point.

Cardioid microphone

CARDIOID MICROPHONE

Microphones are categorized into one of three groups according to directional sensitivity. Omnidirectional microphones pick up sound from a 360-degree field. The omnidirectional microphone is the least valuable for recording bird sounds (because it picks up background sounds as readily as the intended bird sounds), but this microphone is the ideal choice for use in a parabolic reflector. Cardioid microphones eliminate most sound from behind the microphone, but they are not nearly as directional as ultradirectional (shotgun) microphones. Shotgun microphones are ideal for bird sound recording, but high-quality models such as Sennheiser products start at $500 (U.S.).

Parabolic Reflectors

If a bird is vocalizing close to the recorder, even the built-in microphones of certain moderate-priced cassette recorders will succeed in capturing good field recordings. Usually, however, birds are too distant, and there is too much background sound to achieve high-quality recordings with built-in or handheld microphones unless they are of the shotgun design. Parabolic reflectors are much more effective than shotgun microphones and hundreds of times better than a handheld omnidirectional microphone for amplifying sound and increasing directionality and sensitivity. Although parabolas may introduce some distortion, most serious recordists use them because they effectively reduce background sounds by selectively amplifying the desired bird sounds.

There are several drawbacks to parabolas. They can be unwieldy and heavy, especially when held at arm's length for extended periods. Parabolas are better at capturing high-frequency (short wavelength) sounds than low-frequency (long wavelength). A bird song that contains both high-frequency and mid-frequency sounds will be altered when recorded with a parabola, with a relative increase in the amplitude of high frequencies. Low frequencies are limited by the diameter of the parabola. Very low frequency sounds may be picked up by the microphone, but will not be amplified by the reflector, because their wavelengths may be larger than the reflector's diameter.

Parabolic reflector

Parabolas are available in both clear and opaque materials. Clear plastic parabolas have the advantage of permitting the recordist to watch the singing bird through the recording dish. This homemade parabola was built with molded fiberglass. It uses a test tube clamp to hold the microphone in place.

AIMING A PARABOLA

Successful aiming of a parabola in the field requires practice. If the parabola is not aimed accurately at the sound source, the recording will lack the high-frequency content (detail) of the sounds. To aim the parabola correctly, listen through headphones while recording. If the bird is hidden, use the following technique to aim the parabola. First, smoothly pan the parabola across the horizon, beginning at the extreme right or left of where the bird is believed to be, and listen through headphones for the point at which its sound is most clear and loud. Once the correct position on the horizontal axis is found, pan along the vertical axis until you locate the proper elevation. At this point, the parabola will be properly aimed and recording should quickly begin before the bird moves.

Tips for Making Field Recordings

FOCUS ON RECORDING
Leave your camera and telephoto lens behind when making sound recordings. Photography competes with and detracts from the time and patience necessary to make good sound recordings.

GET UP CLOSE
To record bird sounds, approach as close as possible without disturbing the bird. It is just as important to be within close range for recording bird sounds as it is for taking photos.

CHOOSE A QUIET SPOT
Avoid background sounds, such as highway noise and airport traffic by carefully considering these disturbances when selecting a place to record bird sounds.

AVOID DIRECT SUNLIGHT
Never point a parabola with a mounted microphone toward the sun; the reflector will concentrate sunlight and may damage the microphone. Likewise, avoid carrying the parabola over your shoulder if the sun is to your back.

Prairie Warbler

Etiquette for Photographers and Recordists

- Always leave bird nests exactly as you found them, and always leave eggs and young in nests.
- Never keep parents from their nests or young.
- Cover your trail to bird nests as best you can.
- Do not lure rare or locally uncommon birds within photographic range using tape recordings.
- To reduce disturbance to nesting birds, stay in your bird blind for stints of at least one hour.
- Obtain permission before setting up blinds or stalking birds on private land or wildlife sanctuaries.
- To lure distant territorial birds to close recording range, play back the songs of the same bird or those from a prerecorded bird of the same species. To reduce disturbance, do not use this technique continuously or for rare or locally uncommon birds.
- Cameras and microphones offer no privileges to push in front of others or to stalk a bird before everyone in a group is finished watching. It is difficult and usually frustrating to attempt to photograph or record birds while in a group. For these reasons it is usually best to leave your gear at home when joining bird-watching trips.

BRING EARPHONES
Use earphones to aim the parabola with greatest accuracy and to help determine the proper recording level.

A shotgun microphone is the ideal choice for recording birds.

BE AWARE OF WIND
To reduce wind noise, avoid pointing the parabola into the wind and place a windscreen over the microphone recording head.

BRACE YOURSELF
To reduce noises you might make, concentrate on breathing slowly, bracing the parabola, and holding the microphone and earphone cables so that they do not bang against the parabola.

KEEP NOTES
Give your recordings scientific value by including narration on the tape that identifies the bird and provides details about location, date, time, weather, and behavior. Also note the type of recorder and microphone used to make the recording.

LISTEN CAREFULLY
Recognize that even seemingly insignificant sounds such as a mosquito near the microphone or rain falling on the parabola may totally disrupt the recording.

GO EARLY
Bird song is most abundant in early morning, a time when traffic noise and human disturbances are minimal.

CHAPTER FIVE

BIRD FAMILIES OF NORTH AMERICA

There are different approaches to identifying birds. Some field guides group birds by color or by habitat. While useful to consider as part of the identification, such groupings are beset by so many exceptions that they are confusing when applied in nature. The most useful approach is to place an unknown bird into a group of similar-looking birds and use a process of elimination to recognize a specific species. Familiarity with the eighty-seven families of birds common to North America will improve your bird identification skills immeasurably.

FAMILIES, SUB-FAMILIES, AND SPECIES

In the binomial taxonomic system originally devised by Carolus Linnaeus in 1735, all birds are placed in the class Aves, which is subdivided into orders, and then further separated into families (ending in "idae") and subfamilies ("inae"). Subfamilies are sometimes further divided into tribes of related genera which then include species. Ultimately, most birders hope to identify birds to the species level, but some may want to further divide to the subspecies or race distinction. Taxonomists, who study relationships between living things, use studies of anatomy, behavior, and DNA to determine which birds belong to these groups.

The time-honored binomial system of Latin names remains the single most helpful approach for identifying birds. For example, nuthatches compose a distinct family containing 25 species worldwide with 4 species in North America. All members have short tails, straight beaks, and share the habit of moving headfirst down tree trunks. By learning to recognize birds at the family level, one can immediately place an unknown bird in the proper family by the process of elimination. Once you identify the bird's family, consult a local field guide to look for specific field marks. Not all families are as easy to recognize as nuthatches, but the same idea holds; first place unknown birds in the proper families, then use a field guide to focus on specific marks.

This chapter includes bird families in North America; the descriptions cover only the species that occur in North America.

Loons — *Gaviidae*

Loons are the largest diving waterbirds (23-36 inches long) with massive, torpedo-shaped bodies. They can dive to 240 feet, powered by propeller-like legs and webbed feet attached near the tail. Loons usually frequent large lakes, bays, and ocean. Distinguish loons from other waterbirds by their pointed beaks held parallel to the water or angled slightly upward. They can swim with only their heads above the surface. In flight, the neck and beak droop below the plane of the hunchbacked body while feet trail behind. Sexes look alike. **World:** 5 species; **North America:** 5 species.

Loon in flight

Loon on water

Common Loon

Grebes — *Podicipedidae*

Grebes resemble loons; they are diving birds with long necks and pointed bills. Distinguish them by their less massive proportions, longer necks, smaller heads, and rounded, football-shaped bodies. When alarmed, they usually dive rather than take flight. In contrast to loons, they dive only to about twenty feet and stay under for less than a minute. Grebes have a more rapid wingbeat than loons, with narrower wings and trailing legs. When diving, grebes usually throw themselves forward with a graceful roll, or they may submerge slowly. Sexes look alike. **World:** 22 species; **North America:** 7 species.

Grebe in flight

Grebe on water

Western Grebes

Albatrosses — *Diomedeidae*

Albatrosses are enormous seabirds with narrow wings. The family includes the longest-winged birds in the world—some have wingspans of 11.5 feet. Albatrosses have short, thick necks and rounded tails, and glide low over the water on stiff wings, normally landing only to feed or breed. When resting on the water, they sit tilted forward with bills pointed downward. They are rarely sighted from the mainland and few are known from the Atlantic Coast. On the Pacific Coast, Black-footed and Laysan Albatrosses are the most common species, and these regularly occur in offshore waters as far north as Alaska. **World:** 14 species; **North America:** 7 species.

Shearwaters and Petrels — *Procellariidae*

These ocean birds are seldom seen from land, but are often common several miles offshore. They resemble gulls at a distance, but have short tails and flap less frequently. They have long wings that are held stiffly while planing the ocean surface. Within this group, shearwaters have the longest wings; most are dark above and light below, but several species (e.g., Sooty Shearwater) are uniformly dark above and below. Fulmars look more like gulls than shearwaters but are easily distinguished by their stiff, shearwater-like flight habit. Sexes look alike. **World:** 76 species; **North America:** 21 species.

Albatross in flight

Laysan Albatross

Albatross on water

Shearwater on water

Greater Shearwater

Storm-Petrels — *Hydrobatidae*

Storm-Petrels flit like robin-sized swallows over the sea in search of crustaceans and small fish. The storm-petrel family includes some of the most abundant species on earth. Most storm-petrels are dark with white rumps. To identify the various species, consider time of year, distance from mainland, feeding habits, and flight pattern. These are secretive birds on land and all nest on remote islands. Most species return to their underground burrows at night where both sexes (which look identical) share incubation of a single egg and chick-rearing responsibilities. **World:** 21 species; **North America:** 10 species.

Wilson's Storm-Petrel

Storm-Petrel hovering

Tropicbirds — *Phaethontidae*

White-tailed Tropicbird

Tropicbirds are glistening white seabirds with distinctive black patches on wing tips and back. Adults have extraordinary long tail streamers, but these are absent in young. Although they superficially resemble terns, tropicbirds belong to the pelican order. They are best identified by their rapid wingbeats, interrupted by occasional glides. They can twist and turn in flight and capture prey by plunging into the sea. When swimming, they paddle on the surface with cocked tails. In North America, they occur only occasionally along the southeastern and California coasts. **World:** 3 species; **North America:** 3 species.

Tropicbird in flight

Northern Gannet

Boobies and Gannets — *Sulidae*

Gannets are the largest members of this group of diving seabirds. Like other members of the booby family, they are easily recognized by their "pointed look." With pointed wings, beaks, and tails, members of this family are readily distinguished from gulls and are perfectly adapted for plunge-diving in pursuit of fish. Gannets are the most common sulid in North America. Gannets nest in six large colonies in northeastern Canada and winter along the Atlantic Coast and Gulf of Mexico. Tropical boobies compose the remainder of the family and these seldom venture north of the Florida Keys or southern California.
World: 9 species; **North America:** 5 species.

Gannet

Pelicans — *Pelecanidae*

Pelicans are huge waterbirds with massive bodies, thick heads, and oversized beaks. They have a large throat pouch, which they use to capture prey. Although ungainly on land, they are graceful in flight, tucking their heads onto their shoulders in a manner reminiscent of a heron. They often fly in lines or V-formation like geese and may also soar at great heights like vultures. Brown Pelicans can plunge-dive from the air like a gannet; White Pelicans feed from the surface, sometimes cooperatively herding schools of fish into shallow water. **World:** 8 species; **North America:** 2 species.

Brown Pelican

Pelican in flight

Cormorants — *Phalacrocoracidae*

Cormorants have long necks and can swim partially submerged, a habit they share with loons. They are easily distinguished from loons by their tendency to hold their sharply hooked beaks at an upward angle while swimming. When airborne, the cormorant also holds its head above the plane of its body. Unlike most other members of the pelican order, cormorants do not have waterproofed plumage, an adaptation that permits them to quickly lose buoyancy and submerge. After swimming, they frequently hold their wings out to dry. Sexes look alike and both share incubation and chick rearing. **World:** 38 species; **North America:** 6 species.

Cormorant in flight

Cormorant on water

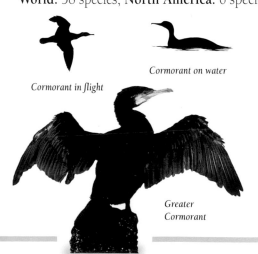

Greater Cormorant

Anhingas — *Anhingidae*

Like cormorants, Anhingas also hold their wings out to dry after pursuing fish. Sometimes called "snakebirds," they have long, curved necks and often swim with only the neck and beak above water, while the body is completely submerged. While swimming, they often fan the long, buff-tipped tail, which gives them another descriptive name, "water turkey." Unlike cormorants, Anhinga sexes look different, with males having a mostly black body; females have a buff-colored head, neck, and breast. In the United States, Anhingas only occur in the southeastern states. **World:** 4 species; **North America:** 1 species.

Anhinga perched

Anhinga in water

Anhinga

Frigatebirds — *Fregatidae*

Frigatebirds are tropical relatives of pelicans capable of effortless, soaring flight. They are named for their habit of stealing food from gulls, boobies, and other hapless providers, much as pirate (frigate) ships plundered for spoil. Recognize frigatebirds by their long, narrow wings with a prominent crook and their deeply forked tail. With wingspans of more than seven feet, the birds are such capable fliers that they may remain airborne for days. In North America, they usually occur in south Florida, the Gulf of Mexico and southern California. **World:** 5 species; **North America:** 3 species.

Magnificent Frigatebird

Herons — *Ardeidae*

Herons are long-legged wading birds found in both fresh and saltwater wetlands. They vary in size from the tiny Least Bittern (about twelve inches) to the Great Blue Heron that stands four feet tall with a seven-foot wingspan. Herons fly with their long necks looped into a graceful curve, head resting between the shoulders and legs trailing. In contrast, cranes, storks, flamingos, and ibis fly with their necks fully extended. White herons are usually called egrets. Bitterns are the best-camouflaged members of the group. Sexes look alike and most species nest together in colonies. **World:** 65 species; **North America:** 16 species.

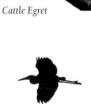

Cattle Egret

Heron in flight

Ibis and Spoonbills — *Threskiornithidae*

Ibis are wading birds with downward curved bills which they use to probe the bottom for crayfish, tadpoles, and fish. They have a strong, direct flight in which they hold their heads and necks stretched forward. Glossy and White-faced ibis look dark in certain lights, but viewed in direct light they glisten with a metallic sheen. Spoonbills have remarkable, spoon-shaped bills which they swing half-open through mud and water, groping for contact with crustaceans and small fish. On contact, spoonbills snap their bills shut on their unsuspecting prey. **World:** 33 species; **North America:** 5 species.

Frigatebird in flight

Ibis

Ibis in flight

Roseate Spoonbill

Storks — *Ciconiidae*

Storks are heavy-bodied wading birds with long necks and featherless heads. Wood Storks are the only North American member of this family. They have slightly drooping bills, but not nearly as decurved as that of an ibis. Wood Storks can soar like vultures at great height and usually feed and nest in groups. Unlike herons, they fly with a fully extended neck and are easily distinguished from soaring White Pelicans because their long legs trail behind. Several storks often feed together, wading belly deep into freshwater wetlands, groping with partly opened bills for frogs, fish, and even small alligators. **World:** 19 species; **North America:** 2 species.

Stork in flight

Wood Stork

Whistling-Duck

Black-bellied Whistling-Duck

Whistling Ducks — *Dendrocygninae*

Whistling-Ducks have long necks and flat-topped heads with steep-rising foreheads. On land, they stand upright and alert on long legs. In flight, they make whistling sounds and have a distinct silhouette as they extend their neck and trail legs clearly beyond the tail. Fulvous Whistling-Ducks occur in salt and brackish marshes from southern California and the Gulf of Mexico to Florida. Black-bellied Whistling-Ducks occur in very southern Texas, often frequenting flooded forests where they sometimes nest in tree cavities. **World:** 8 species; **North America:** 2 species.

Vultures — *Cathartidae*

New World vultures have broad wings, naked heads, and are masters of soaring. Large groups may circle over a carcass or perch in groups for the night. Soaring Turkey Vultures hold their wings in a dihedral, or "V" shape, with gray underwings. In contrast, Black Vultures soar on flat wings, flashing white spots on the wing tips, and have short, squarish tails. The California Condor, the largest land bird in North America, has a wingspan of nine feet. Once widespread in the United States, this species is now extremely rare, restricted to only a few experimentally released birds in southern California and the Grand Canyon. **World:** 7 species; **North America:** 3 species.

Turkey Vulture

Vulture perched

Geese — *Tribe Anserini*

Geese feed mainly on cultivated land, such as farm fields and fertilized lawns or golf courses. At night, most geese roost on water. During the nesting season, females build a nest and lay ten or more eggs, which they incubate as the male stands guard. Sexes look similar, except that the male is larger. Families migrate and spend their first winter together; mated pairs will remain together for many years. **World:** 15 species; **North America:** 9 species.

Goose in flight

Goose

Canada Geese

Swans — *Tribe Cygnini*

In contrast to geese, which graze on land, swans tip upside down with outstretched necks to reach bottom plants in marsh and lake bottoms. Their flight silhouette is unmistakable, identified by the long neck stretched forward with webbed feet tucked against the body. Swans are the only large white water-fowl without black wing tips. Sexes look alike except that males are larger. Trumpeter Swans are the rarest and largest of the three North American species. Like their larger cousin, Tundra Swans migrate in family groups and mate for life. Mute Swans, a species introduced from Europe, can destroy feeding habitat for native swans. **World:** 7 species; **North America:** 4 species.

Swan

Mute Swan

Surface-feeding (Dabbling) Ducks — *Tribe Anatini*

This group is called dabbling ducks for their habit of feeding in shallow water, where they often tip themselves upside down to reach aquatic bottom plants. They often frequent small ponds and marshes and have the ability to make quick takeoffs when disturbed, rather than running across the water, which is the usual take-off pattern for diving ducks. Unlike swans and geese, males and females look very different and do not retain the same mate between years. The group includes many of the most common ducks, such as Mallard, wigeons, and pintail. **World:** 56 species; **North America:** 18 species.

Mallard

Dabbling duck lifting off

Dabbling duck

Diving Ducks — *Tribe Aythyini*

Diving Ducks frequent deep lakes, bays, and oceans where they submerge completely in search of bottom vegetation, fish, and shellfish. Diving ducks must run across the water surface with wings beating furiously in order to become airborne. Males are boldly patterned black and white, usually with iridescence or other colors. Females are earth-toned. The group includes scaups, Redheads, and Canvasbacks. **World:** 17 species; **North America:** 7 species.

Diving duck running across surface of water

Lesser Scaup

Mergansers (and Sea ducks) — *Tribe Mergini*

Merganser in flight

Merganser on water

This group includes sea ducks such as scoters and Harlequin Ducks. This group also includes mergansers, fish-eating ducks with long, thin beaks bearing toothlike serrations. Members of the group are easy to recognize because the females sport distinctive crests. Male Red-breasted and Hooded Mergansers also display bold head feathering. In flight, the merganser holds its head just below the plane of its body, trailing its long, squarish tail. **World:** 7 species; **North America:** 3 species.

Male and female Common Mergansers

Stiff-tailed Ducks — *Tribe Oxyurini*

These small, stocky ducks show the peculiar habit of often holding their stiff tails above their backs. They have thick necks and large, broad bills. They dive like diving ducks and must run across the water to become airborne, but unlike most diving ducks, they often frequent smaller ponds and lakes. The Ruddy Duck is the most common member of this group; Masked Ducks are sometimes found in south Texas and Florida. **World:** 9 species; **North America:** 2 species.

Ruddy Duck

Ruddy Duck

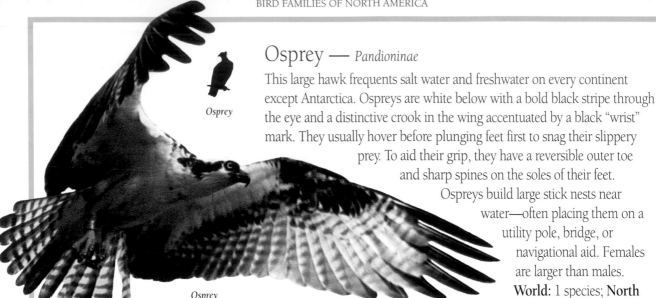

Osprey

Osprey

Osprey — *Pandioninae*

This large hawk frequents salt water and freshwater on every continent except Antarctica. Ospreys are white below with a bold black stripe through the eye and a distinctive crook in the wing accentuated by a black "wrist" mark. They usually hover before plunging feet first to snag their slippery prey. To aid their grip, they have a reversible outer toe and sharp spines on the soles of their feet.

Ospreys build large stick nests near water—often placing them on a utility pole, bridge, or navigational aid. Females are larger than males. **World:** 1 species; **North America:** 1 species.

Eagles —

Eagles resemble massive buteo hawks, with long, broad wings and relatively short tails. Bald Eagles are grouped with sea-eagles and are more closely related to kites than they are to the Golden Eagle, which is kin to the buteos (see opposite). The deliberate wing strokes of Bald Eagles bring to mind a "flapping blanket" effect, but as these grand birds capture rising hot air thermals, they appear to soar effortlessly. In flight, eagles are distinguished from Turkey Vultures because they hold their wings flat, while Turkey Vultures tilt their wings upward. Adult Golden and Bald Eagles have distinctive patterns, but young birds are easily confused because both have white in their wings and tails; it takes four to five years to attain adult plumages. **World:** 22 species; **North America:** 1 species.

Golden Eagle

Eagle perched   *Eagle in flight*

Kites —

Kites are graceful birds of southern latitudes with slender bodies and long wings. All have dark-and-light contrasting plumages. Recognize the Swallow-tailed Kite by its deeply forked tail and contrasting wings. The Snail Kite is slate gray with a white rump. They maintain a diet of large, aquatic snails and are restricted to wetlands in south Florida. Mississippi and Black-shouldered Kites have long, square-tipped tails and falconlike wings. Kites feed mainly on insects, but supplement their diet with rodents, lizards, and snakes. **World:** 20 species; **North America:** 5 species.

Kite

Swallow-tailed Kite

Accipiters —

These are bird-eating hawks of woods and thickets. Their short, rounded wings and long tails give them maneuverability in dense cover. When flying over open country, they usually flap their wings several times followed by a sustained glide. Sharp-shinned Hawks are pigeon-sized accipiters that feed largely on songbirds. These and the crow-sized Cooper's Hawk are the most common birds to take feathered prey at bird feeders. Goshawks are the largest member of the group, capable of taking grouse-sized prey. **World:** 60 species; **North America:** 3 species.

Northern Goshawk

Accipiter

Harriers —

Harriers are slim hawks with long wings and tails. In flight, they hold their wings in a dihedral, reminiscent of how a Turkey Vulture sets its wings. Harriers, once known as Marsh Hawks, typically fly low over fields and wetlands, hovering before dropping to catch mice. They rarely perch in trees or on utility poles. Both sexes display a conspicuous white rump. Adult males are white below with blue-gray upper parts; females and immatures are chocolate brown above. **World:** 13 species; **North America:** 1 species.

Northern Harrier

Harrier

Buteos —

These heavy-bodied hawks have relatively short, rounded wings and broad tails with distinctive striping or colors. Buteos often circle over ridges and hilltops with only an occasional flap of wings as they capture rising warm air. Red-tailed Hawks are the most abundant species in the group and are easily told from other hawks with their dark head, bold white chest, and habit of perching in exposed trees or atop utility poles. Although not in the same genus, Golden Eagles and several closely related tropical hawks (Gray, Black, and Harris's Hawk) are related and share the typical buteo shape. Sexes look similar except that females are larger. **World:** 83 species; **North America:** 15 species.

Red-tailed Hawk

Buteo in flight

Buteo perched

Crested Caracara

Caracara

Caracaras — *Caracarinae*

The Crested Caracara is the only member of this largely tropical subfamily that occurs in the United States. Found only in the southwestern U.S. and central Florida, they are colorful scavengers of open prairie and rangeland. Their conspicuous crest, white face, white wing patches, rump, and neck, and long legs are distinctive. **World:** 10 species; **North America:** 1 species.

Falcons — *Falconinae*

Falcons are the most streamlined of all raptors, with sharply pointed wings and long tails. They have a large-headed, large-shouldered look and often sit on a high perch, where they scan their domain for prey and intruders of their own species. They vary greatly in size and color pattern, from the diminutive American Kestrel (12 in.) to the Gyrfalcon (25 in.); nearly all falcons have a dark streak under the eye. This is most conspicuous in the Peregrine Falcon, which is famed as one of the fastest birds in the world, capable of attaining speeds of 175 mph as it stoops in pursuit of slower-flying birds. **World:** 48 species; **North America:** 8 species.

Falcon in flight

Falcon perched

American Kestrel

Chachalacas — *Cracidae*

Chachalaca

Guans, curassows, and chachalacas are long-tailed members of the galliform order, related to pheasants, grouse, and quail. Most species live in tropical habitats, usually frequenting forest interiors and edges. In addition to long tails and necks, they have chickenlike beaks and strong, walking legs. The Plain Chachalaca is the only species found in the United States and it is restricted to southernmost Texas. Chachalacas receive their name from their call, a piercing *cha-cha-laca,* repeated with rhythm for long periods in chorus. **World:** 50 species; **North America:** 1 species.

Plain Chachalaca

Partridges and Pheasants — *Phasianinae*

Pheasants are slender-bodied members of this chickenlike group—easily recognized by their long tails and small heads. The Ring-necked Pheasant, introduced from China, is the only widely distributed pheasant in North America. Partridges are plump, short-tailed ground birds native to Eurasia. Two introduced partridges are widely established in the western states. These are the Gray Partridge and the Chukar which inhabit agricultural land and barren rocky habitats, respectively. Males are showy; females have camouflaged plumage. **World:** 159 species; **North America:** 4 species.

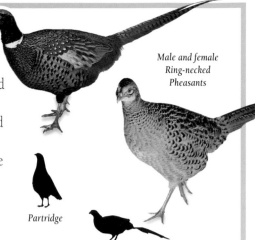

Male and female Ring-necked Pheasants

Partridge

Pheasant

Ruffed Grouse

Grouse — *Tetraoninae*

These chickenlike birds frequent a wide range of habitats across North America. Most grouse species normally live in forested or shrub habitats, prairie chickens occupy grasslands, and ptarmigan live above the tree line in alpine or northern habitats. Many species are especially adapted to cold climates and have dense feathers which extend down to the toes. Males are more boldly patterned than females and often go to great lengths to attract mates by performing elaborate dances accompanied by dramatic booming and drumming sounds. **World:** 17 species; **North America:** 10 species.

Grouse

Turkey — *Meleagridinae*

Wild Turkeys are a slimmer version of the familiar barnyard bird. Recognize them by their large size and habit of parading in open fields in flocks sometimes containing twenty or more birds. Turkeys have bare-skinned heads that brighten with color during the courtship season. Males are larger than females and sport a blue face and neck skin with red wattles. Males spread their fanned tails to impress females and may grow to fifty inches. Females are less iridescent and showy than the males and rarely exceed thirty-seven inches in length. Although turkeys can fly, they prefer to run when threatened. **World:** 2 species; **North America:** 1 species.

Wild Turkey

Turkey

Common Moorhen

Rails, Gallinules, and Coots — *Rallidae*

Most members of the rail family live in marsh habitat where they creep through tangles of dense vegetation. Rails have compressed bodies and long legs and toes which permit them to slip through tight places by pulling the vegetation aside. Most species have cryptic colors and are seldom seen, but their loud calls are distinctive although somewhat ventriloquial. Moorhens (gallinules) and coots are chicken-like members of the rail family. They can swim as well as walk over floating plants. Sexes look alike. **World:** 143 species; **North America:** 14 species.

Rail

New World Quail — *Odontophoridae*

Quail are social birds with rounded bodies, short tails, and small heads. Males are more brightly patterned than females. They live in flocks and usually run when threatened, but may explode into flight as a group. They usually inhabit open meadows with brushy borders. **World:** 30 species; **North America:** 6 species.

California Quail

Quail

Limpkins — *Aramidae*

Limpkins are solitary, nonmigratory wading birds restricted to the Southeast. They frequent freshwater marshes and swamps, feeding mainly on large snails. Closely related to cranes, Limpkins resemble ibis with long necks, legs, and drooping bills. At close range, they are easily recognized by the white spots on neck, breast, and shoulders. Their flight pattern is slow and steady and resembles the shape of a crane because of their outstretched necks. When walking, Limpkins pump their tails up and down in an exaggerated motion, while giving loud, wailing calls, especially at dawn, dusk, and during the night. **World:** 1 species; **North America:** 1 species.

Limpkin

Limpkin

Cranes — *Gruidae*

Cranes are sometimes confused with Great Blue Herons because both have long necks and legs. Cranes are easily distinguished, however, by their habit of flying with necks outstretched—a habit that contrasts with the heron's posture of flying with its head held close to its body. On the ground, North American cranes have a distinctive shape because of a tufted spot over the rump. Standing up to five feet tall, Whooping Cranes are North America's tallest bird. Cranes migrate in "V" formation, much like geese, calling with trumpeting voices that can carry up to a mile. Sexes look alike. **World, 15 species; North America:** 3 species.

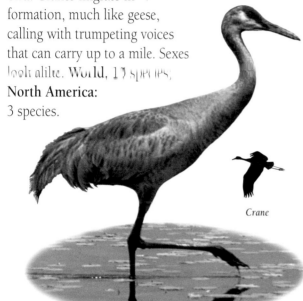

Crane

Sandhill Crane

Plovers — *Charadriidae*

Plovers are round-bodied birds that frequent agricultural fields, grasslands, and shores. In contrast to sandpipers, plovers have large heads and eyes and relatively short beaks that give the head a dovelike appearance. They have short tails and most have the habit of holding their bodies horizontal or at a slight upward angle as they run. The group includes the Killdeer—an abundant species that often nests in agricultural land, baseball fields, and even rooftops. Plovers also include several rare species, such as Piping and Snowy Plovers, that nest on sandy beaches. **World:** 66 species; **North America:** 16 species.

Piping Plover

Plover

American Oystercatcher

Oystercatchers — *Haematopodidae*

Oystercatchers are large, chunky shorebirds with short tails and sturdy walking legs. Their impressive red bills are compressed from the sides and are used to dislodge mollusks, crabs, and marine worms. Oystercatchers usually frequent sandy and rocky marine shores where mollusks abound. They feed on oysters, mussels, and other bivalves soon after the tide falls—before the mollusks have completely closed their shells. The American Oystercatcher is a boldly patterned black-and-white bird with strongly marked wings and tail; the Black Oystercatcher is completely dark with a large, scarlet beak. **World:** 11 species; **North America:** 2 species.

Oystercatcher

Stilts and Avocets — *Recurvirostridae*

Avocets and stilts are graceful shorebirds with bold black and white patterns and extremely slender bills, necks, and legs. They occur in freshwater, alkaline, or brackish shallow wetlands, where they probe for crustaceans, insects, and small fish. Black-necked Stilts have a straight, needlelike bill; American Avocets have a graceful, upward-curving bill, which they sweep back and forth in shallow water. Both species may wade up to their bellies or swim into deeper water. **World:** 10 species; **North America:** 3 species.

Stilt

Avocet

American Avocet

Sandpipers and Phalaropes — *Scolopacidae*

Sandpipers differ from plovers by having longer bills and legs with proportionately smaller heads and eyes. Most sandpipers have brown or gray mottled backs with contrasting white bellies. Some, like Red Knots and Dunlin, are brightly colored in the spring, but molt to drabber colors by fall. Sandpipers usually feed by probing their beaks into mud, but others such as curlews feed on grasshoppers and eat berries. Woodcocks are upland members of the group that feed mostly on earthworms. Phalaropes are the most ocean-going, snapping up plankton from the sea surface miles from land. Sandpipers range in size from the Long-billed Curlew (twenty to twenty-six inches) which has a down-curved eight-inch bill to the tiny Least Sandpiper whose entire body (and bill) may be just five inches long. **World:** 88 species; **North America:** 64 species.

Mixed flock of sandpipers

Dunlin head   *Woodcock head*   *Greater Yellowlegs head*   *Whimbrel head*   *Phalarope*

Jaegers and Skuas — *Stercorariinae*

These hawk-like seabirds have sharply hooked beaks and claws. Skuas are heavy-bodied and resemble gulls. They are dark brown with white patches at the base of their primaries. Skuas prey on eggs and chicks of other seabirds and also scavenge. Jaegars are falconlike predators that feed mainly on rodents and songbirds, sometimes harassing terns to drop their prey or gulls to disgorge a meal. Prior to migration, they may feed on crowberries. **World:** 8 species; **North America:** 5 species.

Jaeger in flight

Parasitic Jaegers

Gulls — *Larinae*

Gulls are masters of flight and are capable at swimming and walking. Combine these talents with quick intelligence and a beak that permits consumption of a diverse diet and it is little wonder that gulls are abundant and widely distributed. "Seagull" is a misnomer; gulls also frequent inland lakes, farms, and even large parking lots where they raid dumpsters for "fast food." Gulls often soar like hawks, but have relatively long wings with flight feathers (primaries) held close together. Gulls take several years to develop adult plumage and show a wide range of mottled browns and grays as they mature. Sexes look alike.
World: 51 species;
North America: 27 species.

Herring Gull

Gull standing

Gull flying

Common Tern

Terns — *Sterninae*

Most terns can be quickly recognized by two key features—forked tails and a black cap. They are masters of grace and agility as they hover over water in search of tiny fish. When hovering, they typically hold their pointed beaks in a sharp downward angle, then plunge just to the water surface. Terns are more streamlined than gulls, with sharply pointed wing tips. Identification of species depends on subtleties of body size, wing color, and details of beak and feet. Terns are highly migratory, traveling deep into the southern hemisphere or at least to southern coastal areas of the U.S. Sexes are alike. **World:** 44 species; **North America:** 19 species.

Tern in flight

Tern perched

Skimmers — *Rynchopinae*

Related to gulls and terns, skimmers have very long black wings, short legs, and extraordinary red beaks which they use to slice through the water in search of fish and crustaceans. Beaks are scissorlike, with a longer lower mandible. Skimmers are found mainly in coastal bays, tidal estuaries, and ocean inlets, where they course in groups just over the water in a swift, graceful flight. In North America, they occur mainly along the southeastern, southwestern, and Gulf coasts. **World:** 3 species; **North America:** 1 species.

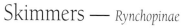

Skimmer skimming

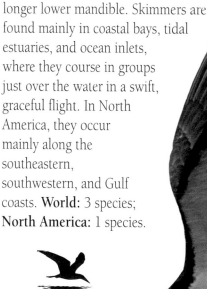

Black Skimmer

Alcids — *Alcidae*

These black-and-white seabirds (also known as auks) live on the ocean most of the year and return to nesting islands during the summer months. In the air, auks have a buzzing flight manner and spread their legs wide on landing. Underwater, the stocky wings function as flippers, permitting impressive dives up to 600 feet deep (murres). The group includes puffins, murres, razorbills, and guillemots, as well as smaller members—auklets and murrelets. Bills vary greatly, but tend to be flattened from the side, especially in the puffins. Sexes look alike. From the mainland, watch for alcids during winter storms or visit their colonies by boat during the summer. **World:** 24 species; **North America:** 22 species.

Common Murre on water

Atlantic Puffins

Pigeons and Doves — *Columbidae*

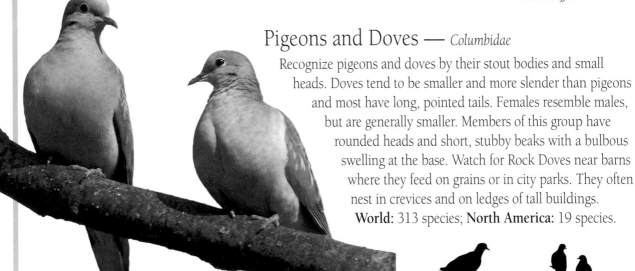
Mourning Doves

Recognize pigeons and doves by their stout bodies and small heads. Doves tend to be smaller and more slender than pigeons and most have long, pointed tails. Females resemble males, but are generally smaller. Members of this group have rounded heads and short, stubby beaks with a bulbous swelling at the base. Watch for Rock Doves near barns where they feed on grains or in city parks. They often nest in crevices and on ledges of tall buildings. **World:** 313 species; **North America:** 19 species.

Rock Dove

Mourning Doves

Parrots — *Psittacidae*

These are large-headed mostly tropical birds with distinctly hooked beaks. Most have green bodies with patches of yellow or red on their heads or wings. Parrots are larger than their more slender relatives, parakeets, which have long, pointed tails. Two species were native to North America. The Carolina Parakeet became extinct in 1920 and the Thick-billed Parrot no longer nests in the southwestern states. Most free-flying parrots in North America are escaped birds from the pet trade. **World:** 358 species; **North America:** 6 species.

Parrot

Monk Parakeet

Cuckoos — *Cuculidae*

Most cuckoos have slender bodies with long tails. Black-billed and Yellow-billed Cuckoos tend to skulk through dense thickets and are more often heard than seen. They make rhythmic, repetitive songs, especially preceding rains—which gives them the common name of "rain crow." The group also includes anis—grackle-sized black birds with extremely long tails—and the Greater Roadrunner, a quick-legged ground bird of the southwestern states. **World:** 142 species; **North America:** 8 species.

Cuckoo

Yellow-billed Cuckoo

Barn Owls — *Tytonidae*

Barn owls are a distinctive group that resemble other owls, but possess smaller eyes and heart-shaped facial disks, which give them a monkey-faced look. Their legs are very long and are covered with bristle-like feathers. In flight, they appear white from below. They nest in caves, hollow trees, barns, under bridges, and in a variety of other human-built structures. **World:** 17 species; **North America:** 1 species.

Barn Owl

Barn Owl

Typical Owls — *Strigidae*

Vertical posture and enormous eyes dominate the appearance of typical owls. The big eyes are surrounded by large facial discs that amplify sound to the hidden ears. Typical owls can be loosely grouped into those with ear tufts and those without. The ear tufts of Great Horned Owls, Long-eared Owls, and screech-owls probably help the birds recognize each other at a distance by creating distinctive silhouettes. Owls such as Barred Owls and Saw-whet Owls lack tufts. Owls are difficult to locate during the day because of their cryptic colors of brown, gray, and buff, but they will often come to recorded calls or even a convincing human imitation. **World:** 171 species; **North America:** 20 species.

Eastern Screech-Owl

Great Horned Owl   *Barred Owl*   *Long-eared Owl*   *Owl in flight*

*Common
Nighthawk*

Goatsucker

Goatsuckers — *Caprimulgidae*

Goatsuckers feed mainly at dusk and at night in
pursuit of large flying insects such as moths and
beetles. The group is related to owls, which they
resemble with large eyes and soft plumage marked
cryptically in shades of brown. Goatsuckers have
feeble feet and barely walk on the ground, even
though they nest on the leafy forest floor or on
rooftops (nighthawks). The goatsuckers' name is
derived from the preposterous legend that the birds
used their enormous gape to milk goats. Most
nightjars are identified by their emphatic calls,
which may sound like their names (e.g., Whip-
poor-will and Poorwill). Look for distinctive white
patches on wings and tails. **World:** 82 species;
North America: 9 species.

Swifts — *Apodidae*

Chimney Swift

Swifts have long,
pointed wings which
give them the
superficial appearance
of swallows, but they
are easily identified by
their stiff wingbeat and
"cigarlike" body shape
that tapers at both
ends, lacking the
swallow's forked or
squared-off tail. Swifts
cling to rock walls, tree
cavities, and chimneys using their sharp claws and
their stiff, proplike tail that is tipped with sharp
spines. Swifts never sit on a branch or walk
on the ground and can sleep, bathe, and
copulate while flying. **World:** 101 species;
North America: 9 species.

*Chimney Swift
in flight*

Hummingbirds — *Trochilidae*

These largely tropical birds are remarkably insect-
like, capable of hovering and even flying backward.
They live in a world of flower blooms, with most
species migrating thousands of miles to insure a
dependable nectar supply supplemented with
appetizers of insects and spiders.
Most hummingbirds are iridescent
green on the back and white below with every
possible gemlike color for throat accent. The Ruby-
throated Hummingbird is the only common species
in the Eastern U.S., but seventeen species occur in
western states, with the greatest variety inhabiting the
southwestern region. **World:** 329 species; **North
America:** 23 species.

Hummingbird in flight

Ruby-throated Hummingbird

Trogons — *Trogonidae*

Trogons are colorful, robin-sized birds with long, squared-off tails, thick necks, and vertical posture. Most species live in tropical latitudes of the Americas, but some are also found in tropical Africa and Asia. The Elegant Trogon is the only species that nests commonly north of Mexico and it is restricted to southeastern Arizona. **World:** 39 species; **North America:** 2 species.

Elegant Trogon

Trogon perched

Hairy Woodpecker

Woodpecker on tree

Woodpecker flight pattern

Kingfisher perched

Belted Kingfisher

Kingfishers — *Alcedinidae*

Kingfishers are large-headed, long-beaked birds with a distinct crest. They are usually solitary and frequent dead snags or utility lines that overhang water. From their favorite perches or a hovering posture, they plunge headfirst into freshwater or salt water to capture small fish and insects. The Belted Kingfisher is the most widespread Kingfisher species in North America. They tunnel burrows into stream banks or quarry cliffs and raise six or seven young. Kingfishers are often heard before they are seen; both sexes give a long, rattling call in flight. **World:** 95 species; **North America:** 3 species.

Woodpeckers — *Picidae*

Woodpeckers cling to tree trunks and hitch themselves upward in short movements, using their stiff tails as a prop. Most woodpeckers fly in a similar manner, a deep undulating flight. In addition to loud calls, woodpeckers communicate their presence and defend territories by distinctive drumming sounds. Most woodpeckers extract ants and other insects from dead wood, but flickers often break this rule by taking ants from the soil. Sexes are similar, except that females usually lack (or have reduced) patches of bright red or yellow on their heads. **World:** 217 species; **North America:** 25 species.

Flycatchers — *Tyrannidae*

Relatively few flycatchers occur in North America and most are small, drab-colored birds that are best identified by their vertical posture and habit of flying out and catching insects in midair. While waxwings share this posture and "hawking" behavior, they are easily distinguished from flycatchers by their singular head tufts. Flycatchers have extremely simple calls that sometimes give rise to common names—such as pewee and phoebe. Within the flycatcher clan, consider size, presence or absence of wing bars, range, and habitat to separate similar species. **World:** 401 species; **North America:** 42 species.

Flycatcher

Eastern Phoebe

Shrikes — *Laniidae*

Shrikes are predatory songbirds that use their hooked beak and strong toes to capture mice, small birds, and insects. North American shrikes have large heads and heavy beaks. At a distance, look for their black mask, wings, and tail. They usually perch on wires or on high snags where they have a good view of the landscape. They store and display their prey on thorns, barbed wire fences, and other conspicuous places where they later return for meals, but the habit may also advertise the hunting prowess of males, an important skill for females to assess when picking a mate. **World:** 30 species; **North America:** 3 species.

Loggerhead Shrike

Shrike

Vireos — *Vireonidae*

Vireos are larger than most warblers, with a more rounded appearance. Most have subtle colors, although a few have bright yellow underparts. They have relatively large heads with stout beaks and a hooked upper mandible used to hold large insects and caterpillars. They typically sit quietly in dense foliage, then sally out to snatch prey from leaves and plant stems. Vireos are easily told from wood warblers by their more sluggish behavior. Use songs, habitat, facial patterns (eye rings and spectacles), and wing bars to separate closely related species. **World:** 52 species; **North America:** 16 species.

Vireo

Blue-headed Vireo

Jays and Crows — *Corvidae*

Crows, jays, and magpies are gregarious birds with complex social orders and diverse languages. They are also generalists—frequenting many habitats and eating diverse foods. Like gulls, most have all-purpose bills and strong walking legs. Crows and their relatives are among the most intelligent birds in the world. Ravens are larger than crows and are distinguished in flight by their wedge-shaped tails and habit of frequent soaring. Jays are the most colorful members of the group; many kinds have iridescent blue backs. Magpies are large black-and-white western birds with long, colorful tails. **World:** 116 species; **North America:** 20 species.

Blue Jay

Blue Jay

Larks — *Alaudidae*

Larks are open-country birds that walk rather than hop. Because perches are scarce in open grasslands, they sing while in flight as they perform elaborate courtship flights. Larks have a high-pitched, musical voice with great carrying power. They often occur in flocks, sometimes mixing with Snow Buntings and longspurs. Sexes are similar. Horned Larks are the only native member of the group—they are more often seen flying away than perched. Watch for their black tails with white outer tail feathers. When perched, they show a distinct black face stripe and chest band. **World:** 91 species; **North America:** 2 species.

Lark

Horned Lark

Swallows — *Hirundinidae*

Swallows are agile, fast-flying , sparrow-sized birds that have pointed wings and short necks. Because they feed mainly on insects, they vacate northern latitudes during winter months. Tail shapes are also useful for identification— many species have notched tails, but only Barn Swallows have deeply forked tails and only Cliff Swallows have squared-off tails. Purple Martins are the largest species; nearly all nest in special housing created by humans. Many species flock together at migration times. **World:** 91 species; **North America:** 14 species.

Barn Swallow

Barn Swallow

Chickadees and Titmice — *Paridae*

Titmice and chickadees are small, active birds with cone-shaped beaks. They have round bodies, fluffy plumage, and live in small groups. They have the habit of feeding while hanging upside down on tree branches or conifer cones and bring this talent to bird feeders where they are very acrobatic visitors. When opening sunflower seeds, they hold each seed between their feet and peck until it cracks. Sexes look alike and all nest in tree cavities and nest boxes. Chickadees have bold black-and-white markings on cap and throat; titmice are mostly gray with a conspicuous crest. **World:** 58 species; **North America:** 11 Species.

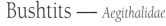

Chickadee perched

Tufted Titmouse

Verdins — *Remizidae*

Verdins are small-bodied birds with short wings and long tails. They are very active, often flitting from one shrub to the next with erratic wingbeats. They are usually solitary except during the nesting season. They build bulky nests that they often use throughout the year for nesting and roosting. Only one species occurs in North America and it is restricted to the low-elevation desert and streamside woodland of the Southwest. **World:** 14 species; **North America:** 1 species.

Verdin

Verdin perched

Bushtits — *Aegithalidae*

Smaller than chickadees, these tiny, long-tailed birds live in scrub oak and other western deciduous forests. Bushtits frequently travel in groups of twenty or more, busily following each other between clumps of vegetation with a characteristic jerky flight. They are usually very vocal when in flocks, often giving a tinkling sound as the flock moves. **World:** 8 species; **North America:** 1 species.

Bushtit perched

Distinctive long tail

Bushtit

Nuthatches — *Sittidae*

Nuthatches are small, lively forest birds with stout bodies and short tails. They are the only birds that have the ability to descend headfirst down tree trunks. Nuthatches have straight or slightly upturned beaks which they use to probe for insects in the furrows of tree bark. Male nuthatches are more brightly colored than females with darker crowns and eye stripes. At feeders they readily take suet and sunflower seeds. They nest in tree cavities and will occasionally use nest boxes. Nuthatches have nasal, repetitive calls with great carrying power. **World:** 25 species; **North America:** 4 species.

Nuthatch on tree

White-breasted Nuthatch

Creepers — *Certhiidae*

Creepers cling to tree trunks much like woodpeckers and nuthatches, but they are easily separated from other tree huggers because of their habit of ascending in a spiral-like manner. Their usual approach is to fly to the base of a tree, spiral upward into horizontal limbs, and then drop to the base of a neighboring tree to repeat the climb. Their brown, mottled plumage offers ideal camouflage against tree bark, their beak has an abrupt downward curve that permits extraction of hidden insects, and their stiff, pointed tail serves as a prop against the trunk. **World:** 7 species; **North America:** 1 species.

Wrens — *Troglodytidae*

Most wrens are small, lively brown birds with round bodies. They have slender, slightly decurved bills and their tails are often cocked over their backs. They have long legs and toes which are often used for scratching among leaves for insects and spiders or for maneuvering through dense vegetation. Wrens vary in size from the eight-inch Cactus Wren to the Winter Wren, which is half that size. They live in nearly all habitats from deserts (Cactus Wren) to shrubby places in backyards (House Wren) to wetlands (Marsh Wren). Songs are usually loud with great carrying power. **World:** 78 species; **North America:** 9 species.

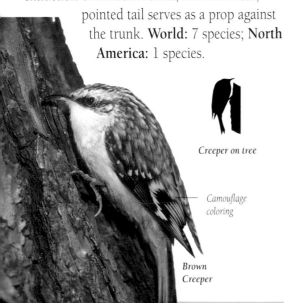

Creeper on tree

Camouflage coloring

Brown Creeper

House Wren

Wren perched

Ruby-crowned Kinglet

Kinglet perched

Dippers — *Cinclidae*

Dippers are sooty-colored, starling-size birds that frequent western mountain streams. They have short wings and stubby tails with extraordinary long legs that help them race among streamside boulders. Dippers have the unique ability among songbirds to dive into fast-flowing streams and fly underwater. They have dense insulation and waterproof plumage maintained by an oil gland that is ten times larger than that found in other birds of the same size. Their name comes from their habit of rapid body bobbing—a behavior that is repeated forty to sixty times per minute. **World:** 5 species; **North America:** 1 species.

Kinglets — *Regulidae*

Kinglets are related to Old World warblers. They are tiny, insect-eating birds with sharp beaks and boundless energy that frequent treetops as well as shrubs. Ruby-crowned Kinglets have loud, musical voices, while the Golden-crowned Kinglet's song consists simply of several high-pitched notes. Head patterns are the best way to distinguish these two species—look for the presence of an eye ring (Ruby-crowned) or eye stripe (Golden-crowned). While perched, they frequently do a nervous wing flit. The colorful crowns that give the Ruby-crowned Kinglets their name are found only on the males and are usually hidden unless the birds become excited. **World:** 6 species; **North America:** 2 species.

American Dipper

Dipper

Old World Warblers — *Sylviinae*

This huge subfamily of insect-eating birds is found mainly in Europe, where most species migrate to Africa. A few species, however, wander from Siberia into Alaska. The Arctic Warbler is the only regular breeder and it is found throughout most of central and western Alaska. Old World warblers resemble the American wood warblers, but lack bright colors. Most are identified by subtle facial and wing marks, distinctive songs, and specific habitat preferences. **World:** 277 species; **North America:** 5 species.

Arctic Warbler

Warbler

Gnatcatchers — *Polioptilinae*

Gnatcatchers are slender, active birds, constantly on the move, flitting between shrubs and forest canopy. Their long tails with white outer feathers are the best clue to identification as they are often cocked over the back like a miniature wren. The several species of gnatcatcher look similar and can best be separated by their ranges. They are often heard before seen as they readily offer their nonmusical banjo-like twangs. The nest is a remarkable structure built of soft plant down that is decorated with lichens held in place with spiderwebs. **World:** 14 species; **North America:** 4 species.

Gnatcatcher perched

Blue-gray Gnatcatcher

Wood Thrush

Thrush

Thrushes — *Turdidae*

Thrushes have large eyes, which help them see in the shadows of forests, and long legs which aid them as they scratch through leaves on the forest floor. Most thrushes have brown backs and speckles or spots on the breast. To separate species, look for eye rings and reddish tints to the tail or head. Robins, bluebirds, and Townsend's Solitaire lack the speckled breast as adults, but both show their family ties in the speckled plumage of young. Song is one of the best ways to detect the presence of this group; each species has a distinctive voice with wonderful musical quality. **World:** 338 species; **North America:** 26 species.

Babblers - *Timaliidae*

The Wrentit is the only member of this Old World family that occurs in North America. It is nearly uniformly gray, with a rounded head and a longish tail, held slightly cocked. It frequents dense tangles along the Pacific coast and would be hard to find if not for its piercing *yip-yip-yip* calls which have a "bouncing ball" quality. Wrentits are related to babblers, a diverse group noted for their loud, vibrant calls. **World:** 267 species; **North America:** 1 species.

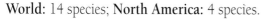

Wrentit perched

Wrentit

Mockingbirds and Thrashers — *Mimidae*

Thrashers and mockingbirds have long bodies and tails. Members of this group also have long legs and toes and either straight or decurved beaks. Most live in dense shrubs and feed on the ground, scratching among leaves to expose hiding spiders, earthworms, and insects. Mockingbirds are the best-known mimics because of their ability to copy the sounds of other birds, but thrashers and catbirds are also proficient at picking up the songs of other species and incorporating phrases into their own songs. **World:** 35 species; **North America:** 12 species.

Thrasher perched

Northern Mockingbird

Pipit

Starlings — *Sturnidae*

Starlings are chunky, active birds with short, pointed wings and tails. They are often seen walking on lawns, probing for insects and seeds. Their color varies from iridescent black in the spring to the star-spangled winter plumage (which gives them their name). Starlings usually occur in huge flocks that may mix with blackbirds. Sexes look similar. European Starlings and Crested Mynas (introduced to Vancouver, British Columbia) are the only two members of this Old World family found in North America. **World:** 114 species; **North America:** 2 species.

American Pipit

Pipits and Wagtails — *Motacillidae*

Pipits are slender birds with long legs adapted for walking and running rather than hopping. They are brown with streaks and have long, thin bills. Pipits nest in Arctic tundra and are most often encountered during migration as they move between the southern U.S. and their summer homes. Watch for flocks in freshly plowed fields or in gravel banks along streams. Wagtails are Old World relatives that occur in Alaska. Both pipits and wagtails have long tails with white outer feathers which they typically lift and then drop. **World:** 63 species; **North America:** 11 species.

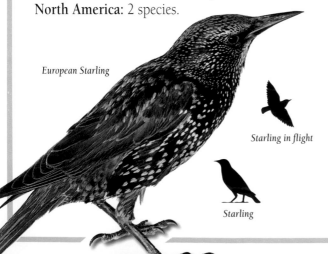

European Starling

Starling in flight

Starling

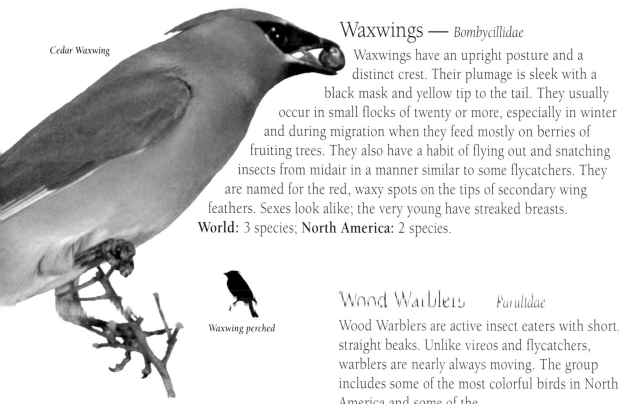

Cedar Waxwing

Waxwings — *Bombycillidae*

Waxwings have an upright posture and a distinct crest. Their plumage is sleek with a black mask and yellow tip to the tail. They usually occur in small flocks of twenty or more, especially in winter and during migration when they feed mostly on berries of fruiting trees. They also have a habit of flying out and snatching insects from midair in a manner similar to some flycatchers. They are named for the red, waxy spots on the tips of secondary wing feathers. Sexes look alike; the very young have streaked breasts. **World:** 3 species; **North America:** 2 species.

Waxwing perched

Wood Warblers — *Parulidae*

Wood Warblers are active insect eaters with short, straight beaks. Unlike vireos and flycatchers, warblers are nearly always moving. The group includes some of the most colorful birds in North America and some of the drabbest. Although a few members are impressive singers, none "warble"; rather they give a variety of " buzzes, trills, chips, and pinks." Warblers favor specific habitats and appear with remarkable regularity during migration and nesting seasons. Identification in the fall is more difficult, when most species lose their brilliant breeding colors, molting into more cryptic tones. **World:** 115 species; **North America:** 57 species.

Yellow Warbler

Silky-flycatchers — *Ptilogonatidae*

Silky-flycatchers are perky birds with a slender shape, upright posture, distinct crests, and long tails. Most species are gregarious, flying in groups with erratic wingbeats, giving the impression of a weak, jerky flight. Most call continuously while in flight. Phainopeplas are the only member of this group that nests in North America. They occur in deserts, wooded river banks, and dry oak forests. Males are jet black; females are gray. Both sexes have distinct crests and flash white in their wings when in flight. **World:** 4 species; **North America:** 2 species.

Phainopepla

Phainopepla perched

Wood Warbler

Tanager perched

Scarlet Tanager

Tanagers — *Thraupidae*

Tanagers are secretive, stout-beaked birds of the forest canopy. This tropical group is represented in North America by a few migratory species. Males take on shades of red during the nesting season, while females are green and yellow. Tanagers hunt insects among the leaves and branches of the canopy but will venture to lower shrubs and forest edges to eat berries and wild fruits. The Scarlet Tanager is the only common tanager of the Northeast; Summer Tanagers occur in the southeastern states and as far north as southern Canada, and Western Tanagers frequent the western mountains and coast. **World:** 249 species; **North America:** 6 species.

Sparrows and Towhees — *Emberizidae*

Sparrows and towhees are ground-feeding birds that frequent a variety of thicket, forest, and open-country habitats. Members of the group use their beaks to crack small seeds and use their long legs and toes to scratch through forest leaves for invertebrates. To identify sparrows, consider the habitat and then look to see if the birds have streaked or unstreaked breasts and if there is a rufous color on the crown. Towhees, juncos, Snow Buntings, and longspurs all have striped young—a reminder of their close relationship to sparrows. **World:** 321 species; **North America:** 59 species.

White-throated Sparrow

Sparrow singing

Cardinals and Allies — *Cardinalidae*

Cardinals; Rose-breasted, Black-headed, and Blue Grosbeaks; Dickcissel; and Lazuli, Indigo, Painted, and Varied Buntings compose a colorful group of birds whose beaks are adapted for taking large-hulled fruits and seeds. During the nesting season, their diets shift to include insects, a higher-protein food necessary for rearing the young. In these species the males are brilliantly colored whereas the females wear tones of brown and buff. These colors signal different roles at the nest, with females doing the incubation and much of the chick rearing, while males mainly defend the territory from intruders. **World:** 43 species; **North America:** 13 species.

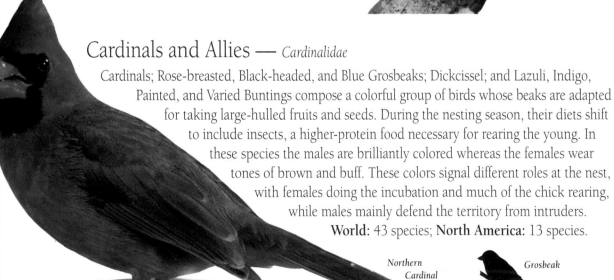

Northern Cardinal

Grosbeak

Blackbirds and Orioles — *Icteridae*

Blackbirds are robin-sized birds that migrate and winter in huge flocks. They have pointed, conical bills and stout walking legs. Grackles are the largest members of the group with long, keel-shaped tails. Wing patches and eye color are key clues to separate Red-winged, Brewer's, and Rusty Blackbirds, which all have moderately long tails. Female blackbirds have muted or striped patterns which provide camouflage at the nest. Meadowlarks and orioles are brightly colored members of the blackbird family. **World:** 98 species; **North America:** 25 species.

Common Grackle

Red-winged Blackbird

Purple Finch

Finches and Allies — *Fringillidae*

Finches are small songbirds with stout, seed-cracking beaks. Males are usually brightly colored; females are streaked or have duller versions of the male plumage. Goldfinches and Purple, House, and Cassin's Finches are common visitors to feeders that offer sunflower seed. "Northern finches," such as Pine and Evening Grosbeaks, Pine Siskins, redpolls, and crossbills, usually feed on seeds extracted from pine, spruce, and other conifers. In years when conifer seed is in short supply, the group is noted for its "irruptive behavior" of moving south to exploit seed at feeders and more southerly conifers. **World:** 170 species; **North America:** 22 species.

Redpoll

Goldfinch

Evening Grosbeak

Crossbill

Old World Sparrows — *Passeridae*

This Old World family has two members introduced to North America—the ubiquitous House Sparrow and the Eurasian Tree Sparrow (found only near St. Louis). Beaks are heavier than for native sparrows, and birds of this family lack the streaking or russet caps. House Sparrows usually cluster in tight groups (often near dumpsters) and frequent urban parks and farmyards. They can weave a communal nest (from dried grasses) but usually nest under building eaves. They also use tree cavities and nest boxes where they compete with native birds such as bluebirds, chickadees, and titmice. **World:** 35 species; **North America:** 2 species.

House Sparrow perched

House Sparrow

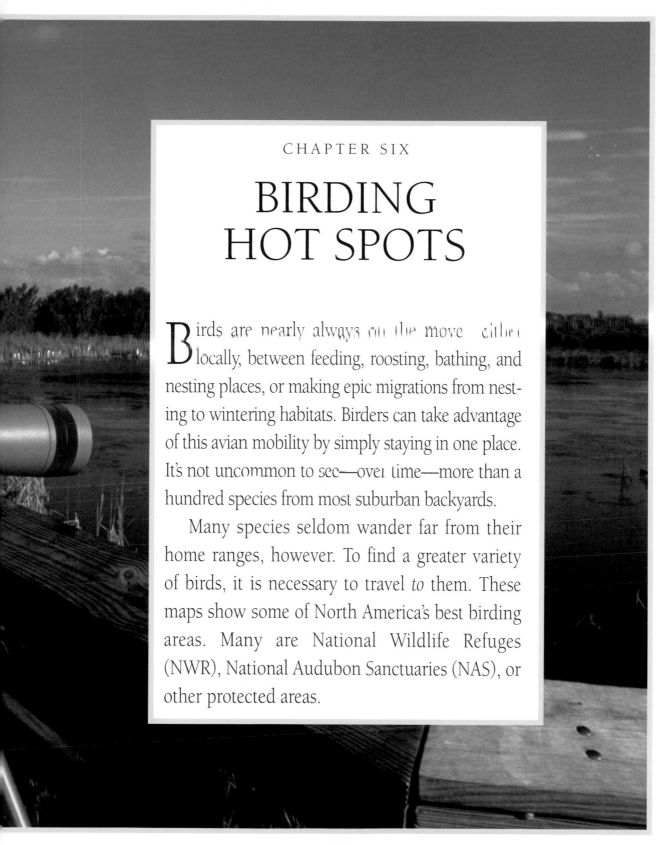

CHAPTER SIX

BIRDING HOT SPOTS

Birds are nearly always on the move—either locally, between feeding, roosting, bathing, and nesting places, or making epic migrations from nesting to wintering habitats. Birders can take advantage of this avian mobility by simply staying in one place. It's not uncommon to see—over time—more than a hundred species from most suburban backyards.

Many species seldom wander far from their home ranges, however. To find a greater variety of birds, it is necessary to travel *to* them. These maps show some of North America's best birding areas. Many are National Wildlife Refuges (NWR), National Audubon Sanctuaries (NAS), or other protected areas.

NORTHEAST

DERBY HILL (Mexico, New York)—An important spring hawk migration location overlooking Lake Ontario. Contact: Derby Hill Observatory, c/o Onondaga Audubon Society, Box 620, Syracuse, NY 13201; hotline March-May, phone: 315-963-8291.

MONTEZUMA NWR (Seneca Falls, New York)—Great flocks of Canada and Snow Geese stage here during migration along with thousands of ducks. Bald Eagles and Ospreys nest at the refuge. Contact: Montezuma NWR, 3395 Route 5 + 20, East Seneca Falls, NY 13148; phone: 315-568-5987.

NIAGARA RIVER (Niagara Falls, Ontario and New York)—The area below the falls is famous for concentrations of gulls from mid-November to mid-January when eighteen species of gulls and thousands of waterfowl congregate. Contact: NYS Parks, Recreation and Historic Preservation; phone: 716-278-1780. Also contact motels in Niagara Falls, Ontario.

HAWK MOUNTAIN (Kempton, Pennsylvania)—An average of 24,000 hawks migrate past this sanctuary from mid-August to December. It features trails, promontories, internships, lectures, and a visitors' center. Contact: Hawk Mountain, 1700 Hawk Mountain Road, Kempton, PA 19529-9449; phone: 610-756-6000.

EDWIN B. FORSYTHE (BRIGANTINE) NWR (Absecon, New Jersey)—Wading birds and shorebirds abound in brackish water impoundments and adjacent salt marsh. Contact: Edwin B. Forsythe NWR, Box 72, Oceanville, NJ 08231; phone: 609-652-1665.

CAPE MAY (New Jersey)—Land birds (especially warblers) congregate here during fall migration, and sixteen hawk species are readily seen. Contact: Cape May Bird Observatory, P.O. Box 3, 701 East Lake Drive, Cape May Point, NJ 08210; phone: 609-861-0700.

BONAVENTURE ISLAND (Perce, Quebec)—North America's largest Northern Gannet colony and home to Common Murres, Black-legged Kittiwakes, and other seabirds. Contact: Tourisme Quebec, P.O. Box 979, Montreal, PQ, Canada H3C 2W3; phone: 514-873-2015.

WITLESS BAY (Bauline, Newfoundland)—Impressive colonies of Atlantic Puffins, Common Murres, and Black-legged Kittiwakes can be viewed on Great, Gull, and Green Islands. For information about Witless Bay and Newfoundland's other protected areas; contact: Parks and Natural Areas Division, 2nd Floor, West Block, Confederation Building, P.O. Box 8700, St. John's, Newfoundland A1B 4J6; phone: 709-729-2424; boat tour contacts: 1-800-563-NFLD.

BRIER ISLAND (Digby, Nova Scotia)—Land birds and shorebirds concentrate on this peninsula during fall migration, and pelagic seabirds are common. For motels, ferry, and pelagic tour schedules, contact: Nova Scotia and New Brunswick tourist offices at 1-800-565-0000 and 1-800-561-0123, respectively.

EASTERN EGG ROCK (New Harbor, Maine)—Atlantic Puffins, Arctic, Common, and Roseate Terns, Black Guillemots, and other seabirds. Contact: Hardy Boat, 1-800-2-PUFFIN (New Harbor, ME) or R.N. Fish and Son; phone:207-633-2626 (Boothbay Harbor, ME).

PARKER RIVER NWR AND PLUM ISLAND (Newburyport, Massachusetts)—Excellent habitat for shorebirds and gulls; also winter alcids after storms; Snowy Owls frequent beaches in most winters. Contact: Parker River NWR, 261 Northern Boulevard, Plum Island, Newburyport, MA 01950; phone: 978-465-5753

MONOMOY NWR (Chatham, Massachusetts)—Important nesting habitat for Piping Plovers, Common and Roseate Terns, and great numbers of shorebirds. Contact: Great Meadows NWR, Sudbury Road, Concord, MA 01742; phone: 617-369-5518.

BLOCK ISLAND (Pt. Judith, Rhode Island)—Land bird stopover during migrations and waterbirds in the winter. Contact: Block Island Chamber of Commerce, Drawer D, Water Street, Block Island, RI 02807; phone:1-800-383-2474.

JAMAICA BAY (New York, New York)—Shorebirds, wading birds, terns, skimmers, and land birds are very accessible to New York City. Contact: Gateway National Recreation Area, Floyd Bennett Field, Brooklyn, NY 11234; phone: 718-338-3338.

SOUTHEAST

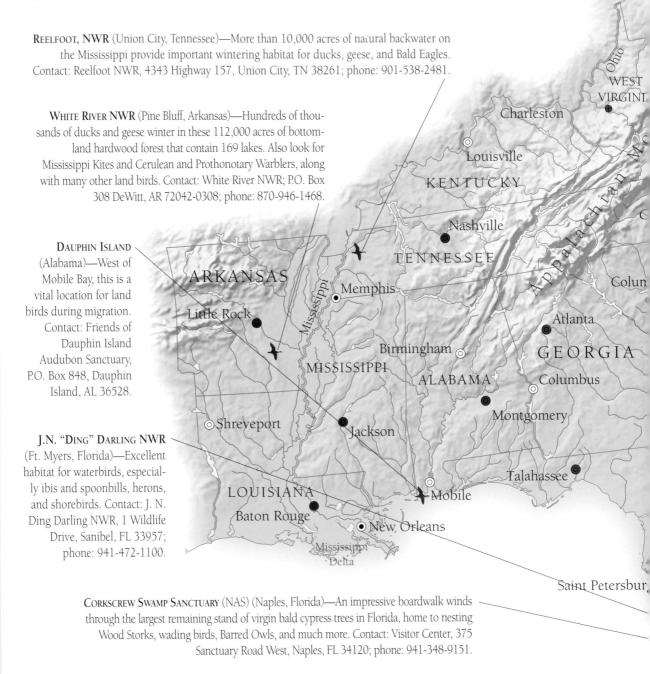

REELFOOT, NWR (Union City, Tennessee)—More than 10,000 acres of natural backwater on the Mississippi provide important wintering habitat for ducks, geese, and Bald Eagles. Contact: Reelfoot NWR, 4343 Highway 157, Union City, TN 38261; phone: 901-538-2481.

WHITE RIVER NWR (Pine Bluff, Arkansas)—Hundreds of thousands of ducks and geese winter in these 112,000 acres of bottomland hardwood forest that contain 169 lakes. Also look for Mississippi Kites and Cerulean and Prothonotary Warblers, along with many other land birds. Contact: White River NWR; P.O. Box 308 DeWitt, AR 72042-0308; phone: 870-946-1468.

DAUPHIN ISLAND (Alabama)—West of Mobile Bay, this is a vital location for land birds during migration. Contact: Friends of Dauphin Island Audubon Sanctuary, P.O. Box 848, Dauphin Island, AL 36528.

J.N. "DING" DARLING NWR (Ft. Myers, Florida)—Excellent habitat for waterbirds, especially ibis and spoonbills, herons, and shorebirds. Contact: J. N. Ding Darling NWR, 1 Wildlife Drive, Sanibel, FL 33957; phone: 941-472-1100.

CORKSCREW SWAMP SANCTUARY (NAS) (Naples, Florida)—An impressive boardwalk winds through the largest remaining stand of virgin bald cypress trees in Florida, home to nesting Wood Storks, wading birds, Barred Owls, and much more. Contact: Visitor Center, 375 Sanctuary Road West, Naples, FL 34120; phone: 941-348-9151.

DRY TORTUGAS (Key West, Florida)—Located 68 miles southwest of Key West, this island outpost is a concentration point for land bird migrants in late April-early May. Audubon's Shearwater, Masked Booby, Magnificent Frigatebird, Sooty Tern, and Brown Noddy are common species. Contact: Site Supervisor, Dry Tortugas National Park, PO Box 6208, Key West, FL 33041; phone: 305-242-7700.

CHINCOTEAGUE NWR (Virginia)—Waterfowl, wading birds, and shorebirds, as well as many common land birds can be seen here. Contact: Refuge Headquarters, P.O. Box 62, Chincoteague, VA 23336; phone: 804-336-6122.

PEA ISLAND NWR (Manteo, North Carolina)—This long finger of land is located within Cape Hatteras National Seashore. It is the winter home for Greater Snow Geese, and wading birds such as egrets and Glossy Ibis nest in the sanctuary. Contact: Refuge Headquarters, 708 North Highway 64, Manteo, NC 27954; phone: 919-987-2394.

FRANCIS BEIDLER FOREST SANCTUARY (NAS) (Harleyville, South Carolina)—Largest known tract of virgin tupelo/bald cypress. Home to Barred Owls, Prothonotary Warblers, and wading birds. Contact: Visitor Center, 336 Sanctuary Road, Harleyville, SC 29448; phone: 803-462-2160.

SAVANNAH NWR (Savannah, Georgia)—This vast refuge of salt marsh and barrier islands is home to Clapper Rails, Painted Buntings, and thousands of Wood Ducks. Contact: Savannah Coastal Refuges, 1000 Business Center Drive, Suite 10, Savannah, GA 31405; phone: 912-652-4415.

OKEFENOKEE SWAMP NWR (Savannah, Georgia)—This 376,000-acre refuge is a mix of freshwater marsh, pine uplands, and dozens of lakes. Sandhill Cranes court on the wet prairies, and Chuck-will's Widows and Prothonotary Warblers are common. Contact: Okefenokee NWR, Route 2, Box 3330 Folkston, GA 31537; phone: 912-496-7366.

MERRITT ISLAND NWR (Orlando, Florida)—Adjacent to the Canaveral Space Center, this 139,305-acre refuge provides habitat for Wood Storks, Clapper Rails, and many wading birds and shorebirds, as well as spectacular land bird migrations in spring and fall. Contact: Merritt Island NWR, P.O. Box 6504, Titusville, FL 32782; phone:407-861-0667.

ARCHBOLD BIOLOGICAL STATION (Lake Placid, Florida)—Interior upland habitats for Scrub Jays and other wildlife of the Lake Wales Ridge. Contact: P.O. Box 2057, Lake Placid, FL 33862-2057; phone 941-465-2571.

LOXAHATCHEE NWR (Boynton Beach, Florida)—The northern remnant of the Everglades with Snail Kites, Limpkins, Fulvous Whistling Ducks, Purple Gallinules, and many shorebirds. Contact: Arthur R. Marshall Loxahatchee NWR, 10216 Lee Road, Boynton Beach, FL 33437-4796; phone: 561-732-3684.

EVERGLADES NATIONAL PARK (Homestead, Florida)—Spans 2,100 square miles of expansive saw grass prairies, broken by islands of subtropical trees, freshwater rivers, and brackish mangrove swamps. Anhingas, spoonbills, herons, ibis, Limpkins, and Swallow-tailed Kites are common. Contact: Everglades National Park, 40001 State Road 9336, Homestead, FL 33034-6733; phone: 305-242-7700.

CENTRAL

AGASSIZ NWR (Thief River Falls, Minnesota)—More than twenty lakes provide summer habitat for sixteen species of ducks and geese. During migration, the refuge supports large numbers of Rough-legged Hawks, Tundra Swans, and many shorebirds and land birds. Contact: Agassiz NWR, Route 1, Box 74, Middle River, MN 56737; phone: 218-449-4115.

DES LACS NWR (Minot, North Dakota)—The prairie pothole lakes of this 18,881-acre refuge provide nesting habitat for Eared and Western Grebes, Black Terns, and many waterfowl. The prairie grasslands are home to Sharp-tailed Grouse and Sprague's Pipits, as well as Le Conte's and Baird's Sparrows. Contact: Des Lacs NWR, P.O. Box 578, Kenmare, ND 58746-0578; phone: 701-385-4046.

LACREEK NWR (Rapid City, Lacreek)—This 16,147-acre refuge of marsh and grassland is home to Trumpeter Swans, White Pelicans, and Double-crested Cormorants. American Bitterns are common and share their habitat with American Avocets, Forester's and Black Terns, Western Grebes, Black-crowned Night-Herons, and many waterfowl. Contact: Lacreek NWR, HC 5 Box 114, Martin, SD 57551; phone: 605-685-6508.

FORT NIOBRARA NWR (Chadron, Nebraska)—Sharp-tailed Grouse are abundant in the extensive grassland habitat, along with Greater Prairie Chickens, Upland Plovers, Long-billed Curlews, Rock Wrens, and many others. Contact: Fort Niobrara NWR, Ft. Niobrara/Valentine NWR, Complex HC 14, Box 67, Valentine, NE 69201; phone: 402-376-3789.

CRESCENT LAKE NWR (Alliance, Nebraska)—Eighteen ponds and lakes and extensive dunes provide habitat on this 45,818-acre refuge for Sharp-tailed Grouse, Long-billed Curlews, Upland Sandpipers, Wilson's Phalaropes, and many other prairie species. Contact: Crescent Lake NWR HC 68 Box 21, Ellsworth, NE 69340; phone: 308-762-4893.

PLATTE RIVER- LILLIAN ANNETTE ROWE SANCTUARY (NAS) (Grand Island, Nebraska)—About 500,000 Sandhill Cranes congregate in mid-March along a 150-mile stretch of the Platte River, a staging place on their return to arctic nesting grounds. Contact: Sanctuary Manager, 44450 Elm Island Road, Gibbon, NE 68840; phone: 308-468-5282.

CHEYENNE BOTTOMS (Great Bend, Kansas)—This is the major area of shorebird concentration in the central United States. The area hosts at least 39 species during spring and fall migration when as many as 600,000 shorebirds congregate. Contact: Cheyenne Bottoms Wildlife Area, 56 Northeast 40 Road, Great Bend, KS 67530; phone: 316-793-7730.

CHURCHILL, MANITOBA—This small seaport on Hudson Bay is an accessible sample of the vast tundra habitat. Expansive, treeless tundra, broken by countless ponds, provides nesting habitat for shorebirds, seabirds, and land birds. Accessible by rail (204-675-2241) and air (204-675-8851). Contact: Churchill Chamber of Commerce at 204-675-2022.

HORICON MARSH NWR (Madison, Wisconsin)—Noted for huge wintering numbers of Canada Geese, this refuge is also home to thousands of herons and egrets and upland habitat for migrant warblers and other land birds. Contact: Horicon NWR, W4279 Headquarters Road, Mayville, WI 53050; phone: 920-387-2658.

GRAYLING, MICHIGAN—The young jack pines in the vicinity of Grayling are the main nesting area for the endangered Kirtland's Warbler. Contact: U.S. Fish and Wildlife Service at 517-337-6650 or U.S. Forest Service at 517-826-3252.

SHIAWASSEE NWR (Flint River, Michigan)—Thousands of Tundra Swans stop over each spring, along with thousands of ducks, geese, and shorebirds. Great Blue Herons and Bald Eagles nest at the refuge. Contact: Shiawassee NWR, 6975 Mower Road, Saginaw, MI 48601; phone: 517-777-5930.

POINT PELEE NATIONAL PARK, ON—This 6,002-acre point projecting southward into Lake Erie about forty miles southeast of Detroit is famous for concentrations of spring land bird migrants. Contact: Friends of Point Pelee, RR1, Leamington, ON N8H 3V4; phone: 519-322-2365, recorded daily message: 519-322-2371.

OTTAWA NWR (Toledo, Ohio)—The remnant of a vast marsh system, Ottawa still has virgin patches of black swamp woods, providing habitats for waterfowl and migrant land birds. Great Blue Herons and Black-crowned Night-Herons are common and nest on nearby islands. Contact: Ottawa NWR, 14000 West State Route 2, Oak Harbor, OH 43449; phone: 419-898-0014.

DESOTO NWR (Missouri Valley, Iowa)—As many as 400,000 Snow and White-Fronted Geese and a million ducks have concentrated in some years at DeSoto NWR during fall migration, along with many Bald Eagles, which winter here from November to March. Contact: DeSoto NWR, 1434 316th Lane, Missouri Valley, IA 51555-7033; phone: 712-642-4121.

FLINT HILLS NWR (Topeka, Kansas)—In the fall, 100,000 waterfowl can congregate here along with hundreds of White Pelicans and Snowy Egrets. The uplands are home to Dickcissels, Orchard Orioles, Grasshopper Sparrows, and Red-headed Woodpeckers. Contact: Flint Hills NWR, P.O. Box 128, 530 W. Maple, Hartford, KS 66854; phone:316-392-5553.

SOUTHWEST

MONTEREY BAY (California)—A pelagic trip on Monterey Bay can provide views of Flesh-footed and Buller's Shearwaters as well as Ashy and Black Storm-Petrels. Black-footed Albatrosses are a regular on this trip as well as Northern Fulmars, Common Murres, Pigeon Guillemots, and Cassin's and Rhinoceros Auklets. Contact: Shearwater Journeys, P.O. Box 1445, Soquel, CA 95073; phone: 408-688-1990.

SANTA CRUZ ISLAND (Ventura, California)—Santa Cruz Island is where endemic Scrub Jays and Allen's Hummingbirds are found. On the trip to the island, watch for Pink-footed, Sooty, and Black-vented Shearwaters, Black Storm-Petrels, and jaegers. Phone: Island Packers Company, 805-642-1393.

JOSHUA TREE NATIONAL PARK (California)—Located 140 miles east of Los Angeles, Joshua Tree spans two desert types, the Colorado and Mojave Deserts. Desert birds include Bendire's Thrasher, Ladder-backed Woodpecker, and Scott's Oriole. An excellent spot during migration. Many eastern vagrants accidentally end up here. Contact: Park Headquarters, 74485 National Park Drive, Twentynine Palms, CA 92277.

SALTON SEA NWR (California)—This 375-square-mile "sea" is the largest inland body of water west of the Rockies. It is the winter home for huge populations of waterfowl, grebes, wading birds, shorebirds, swallows, warblers, and orioles. Many birds also use it during migration and for nesting. Contact: Salton Sea NWR, 906 West Sinclair Road, Calipatria, CA 92233-0120; phone: 760-348-5278.

MADERA CANYON (Green Valley, Arizona)—The ravines and picnic areas of Madera Canyon offer habitat in huge sycamore trees for an unusual assemblage of birds that are most often associated with Mexico. Watch for the Elegant Trogon, Suphur-bellied Flycatcher, Painted Redstart, Scott's Oriole, Hepatic Tanager, and Mexican Junco, among many others. Contact: Chamber of Commerce, 465 W Saint Marys Road, Tucson, AZ , 85701-8299; phone: 520-792-1212.

RAMSEY CANYON PRESERVE AND HUACHUCA MOUNTAINS—Large numbers of hummingbirds visit feeders. Contact: Nature Conservancy Arizona Field Office, 300 E. University Boulevard, Suite 230 Tucson, AZ 85705; phone: 520-378-2785.

SONOITA CREEK SANCTUARY (Patagonia, Arizona)—This small sanctuary (just 312 acres) is legendary among birders. The extensive land bird list includes remarkable diversity, including many Mexican birds. Contact: Nature Conservancy Arizona Field Office, 300 E. University Boulevard, Suite 230, Tucson, AZ 85705; phone: 520-622-3861.

CHIRICAHUA NATIONAL MONUMENT (Willcox, Arizona)—Evergreen oak woodlands, sycamores, and grasslands provide habitat for a diverse group of land birds including Blue-throated and Broad-tailed Hummingbirds, Gray-breasted Jays, Mexican Chickadees, Grace's Warblers, Painted Redstarts, and Hepatic Tanagers. Contact: HCR2 Box 6500, Willcox, AZ 85643; phone: 520-824-3560.

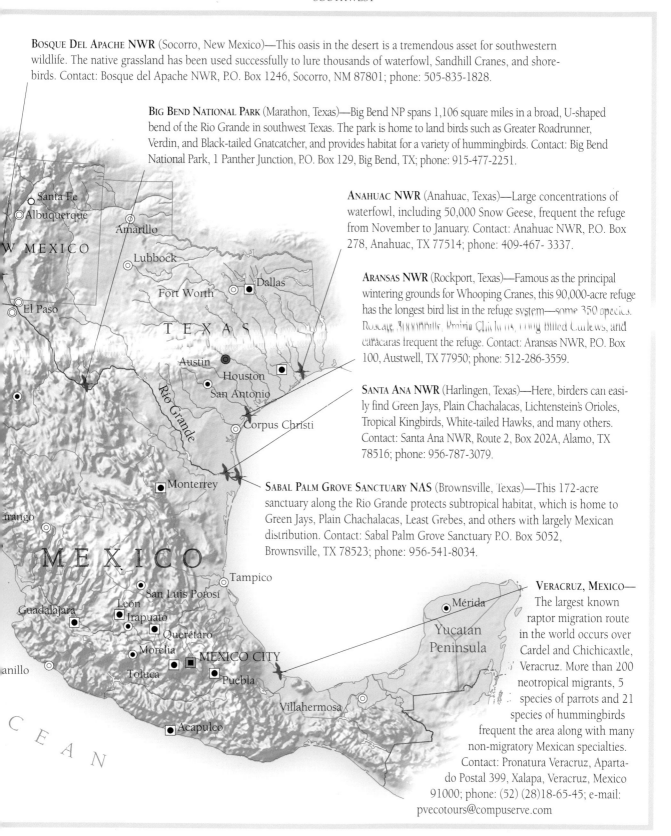

BOSQUE DEL APACHE NWR (Socorro, New Mexico)—This oasis in the desert is a tremendous asset for southwestern wildlife. The native grassland has been used successfully to lure thousands of waterfowl, Sandhill Cranes, and shorebirds. Contact: Bosque del Apache NWR, P.O. Box 1246, Socorro, NM 87801; phone: 505-835-1828.

BIG BEND NATIONAL PARK (Marathon, Texas)—Big Bend NP spans 1,106 square miles in a broad, U-shaped bend of the Rio Grande in southwest Texas. The park is home to land birds such as Greater Roadrunner, Verdin, and Black-tailed Gnatcatcher, and provides habitat for a variety of hummingbirds. Contact: Big Bend National Park, 1 Panther Junction, P.O. Box 129, Big Bend, TX; phone: 915-477-2251.

ANAHUAC NWR (Anahuac, Texas)—Large concentrations of waterfowl, including 50,000 Snow Geese, frequent the refuge from November to January. Contact: Anahuac NWR, P.O. Box 278, Anahuac, TX 77514; phone: 409-467-3337.

ARANSAS NWR (Rockport, Texas)—Famous as the principal wintering grounds for Whooping Cranes, this 90,000-acre refuge has the longest bird list in the refuge system—some 350 species. Roseate Spoonbills, Prairie Chickens, Long-billed Curlews, and caracaras frequent the refuge. Contact: Aransas NWR, P.O. Box 100, Austwell, TX 77950; phone: 512-286-3559.

SANTA ANA NWR (Harlingen, Texas)—Here, birders can easily find Green Jays, Plain Chachalacas, Lichtenstein's Orioles, Tropical Kingbirds, White-tailed Hawks, and many others. Contact: Santa Ana NWR, Route 2, Box 202A, Alamo, TX 78516; phone: 956-787-3079.

SABAL PALM GROVE SANCTUARY NAS (Brownsville, Texas)—This 172-acre sanctuary along the Rio Grande protects subtropical habitat, which is home to Green Jays, Plain Chachalacas, Least Grebes, and others with largely Mexican distribution. Contact: Sabal Palm Grove Sanctuary P.O. Box 5052, Brownsville, TX 78523; phone: 956-541-8034.

VERACRUZ, MEXICO— The largest known raptor migration route in the world occurs over Cardel and Chichicaxtle, Veracruz. More than 200 neotropical migrants, 5 species of parrots and 21 species of hummingbirds frequent the area along with many non-migratory Mexican specialties. Contact: Pronatura Veracruz, Apartado Postal 399, Xalapa, Veracruz, Mexico 91000; phone: (52) (28)18-65-45; e-mail: pvecotours@compuserve.com

NORTHWEST

MALHEUR NWR (Burns, Oregon)—This grand refuge encompasses 282 square miles of marsh, high desert, ponds, and lakes, and provides habitat for 260 species of birds. More than 40,000 avocets and many shorebirds migrate through, and Greater Sandhill Cranes court and stage here during migration. Contact: Malheur NWR, HC 72, Box 245, Princeton, OR 97721-9505; phone: 541-493-2612.

WILLIAM L. FINLEY NWR (Oregon)—The fertile Willamette Valley provides wetland and upland habitat for many species, including the rare Dusky Canada Goose, whose entire population winters here. An interpretive hiking trail offers opportunities for birders to see upland birds, such as California Quail, thrushes, and warblers. Contact: William L. Finley NWR, c/o Western Oregon Complex, 26208 Finley Refuge Road, Corvallis, OR 97333-9533; phone: 541-757-7236.

HUMBOLT BAY NWR (California)—This refuge is an important stopover for most of the Pacific coast Brant Geese, which number about 200,000. This 8,600-acre sanctuary may host 150,000 shorebirds in midwinter and is home for the second largest colony of Great Blue Herons and egrets in California. Contact: Humboldt Bay NWR, 1020 Ranch Road, Loleta, CA 95551-9633; phone: 707-733-5406.

SACRAMENTO NWR (Willows, California)—This 11,000 acres of wetlands is winter home to 300,000 geese and a million or more ducks. The refuge is also home to Yellow-billed Magpies, Barn Owls, White-tailed Kites, and many land birds, especially White-crowned and Golden-crowned Sparrows. Contact: Sacramento NWR, 752 County Road, 99W Willows, CA 95988-9639; phone: 530-934-2801.

YOSEMITE NATIONAL PARK (Merced, California)—The grandeur of Yosemite Valley is complemented by its abundance of birdlife. Even the most frequented locations, such as the forested picnic areas, are frequented by common birds such as Steller's Jays, Western Tanagers, woodpeckers, and juncos. Golden Eagles and White-throated Swifts are often seen overhead. Contact: Yosemite National Park, P.O. Box 577, Yosemite, CA 95389; phone: 209-372-0200.

DON EDWARDS (SAN FRANCISCO BAY) NWR (Fremont, California)—The refuge is home to at least half of the endangered California Clapper Rails. Birders can also have excellent views of White-tailed Kites, avocets, stilts, and thousands of other shorebirds and wading birds. Contact: Don Edwards San Francisco Bay NWR, c/o San Francisco Bay Complex, P.O. Box 524, Newark, CA 94560-0524; phone: 510-792-0222.

NISQUALLY NWR (Washington)—Located near two million people, this 1,796-acre refuge is on a delta in the mouth of Puget Sound. The refuge is the winter home for thousands of seabirds, shorebirds, and waterfowl. Also visit Dungeness, a 5-mile-long sand spit extending into the Strait of Juan de Fuca. Contact: Nisqually NWR, 100 Brown Farm Road, Olympia, WA 98516-2302; phone: 360-753-9467.

CHARLES M. RUSSELL NWR (Montana)—This nearly one-million-acre refuge is home to Mountain Plovers and Burrowing Owls which nest within vast prairie dog colonies. Sharp-tailed and Sage Grouse court and nest here during spring. Breeding birds include Golden Eagles, Sandhill Cranes, and many land birds of prairie and forested ravines. Contact: Charles M. Russell NWR, P.O. Box 110, Lewistown, MT 59457; phone: 406-538-8706.

MEDICINE LAKE NWR (Culbertson, Montana)—This 31,170-acre refuge is home to thousands of White Pelicans, and Eared, Horned, and Western Grebes. In the fall, Sandhill Crane numbers may build to 50,000, and up to 200,000 Franklin's Gulls congregate, along with 250,000 waterfowl. Contact: Medicine Lake NWR, 223 North Shore Road, Medicine Lake, MT 59247-9600; phone: 406-789-2305.

SNAKE RIVER BIRDS OF PREY NATIONAL CONSERVATION AREA (Boise, Idaho)—One of the world's densest populations of nesting birds of prey, including eagles, hawks, falcons, owls, and vultures. The area covers 483,000 acres along 81 miles of the Snake River. Contact: National Bureau of Land Management, Boise Field Office, 348 Development Ave., Boise ID 83705; phone: 208-384-3300.

GRAYS LAKE NWR (Soda Springs, Idaho)—This 15,000-acre refuge is located on a high plateau surrounded by the Caribou Mountains. It is home to Bald and Golden Eagles and Prairie Falcons. Breeding water birds include Franklin's and California Gulls, Long-billed Curlews, White-faced Ibis, and Greater Sand Hill Cranes. Contact: Grays Lake NWR, 74 Grays Lake Rd., Wayan, ID 83285-5006; phone: 208-574-2755.

ALAMOSA NWR (Pueblo, Colorado)—This 10,356-acre refuge is located at 7,500 feet, resulting in habitats similar to those found further north in the Dakotas. Bald and Golden Eagles winter at Alamosa and gorge on the abundant fish. The habitat is very good for Black Terns, Wilson's Phalaropes, Black Skimmers, avocets, waterfowl, and wading birds in wetlands and meadows. Contact: Bear River Migratory Bird Refuge, 58 South 950th, West Brigham City, UT 84302; phone: 435-723-5887.

ALASKA & HAWAII

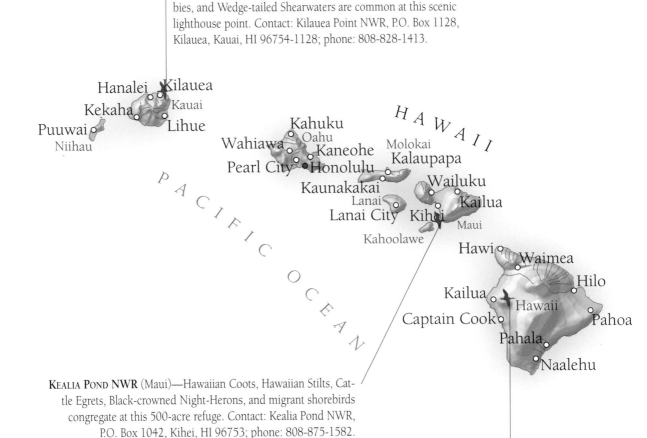

KILAUEA PT. NWR (Hawaii)—Laysan Albatross, Red-footed Boobies, and Wedge-tailed Shearwaters are common at this scenic lighthouse point. Contact: Kilauea Point NWR, P.O. Box 1128, Kilauea, Kauai, HI 96754-1128; phone: 808-828-1413.

Hanalei Kilauea
Kekaha   Kauai
Puuwai   Lihue
Niihau

Kahuku
Wahiawa   Oahu
Kaneohe   Molokai
Pearl City   Honolulu   Kalaupapa
Kaunakakai   Wailuku
Lanai   Kailua
Lanai City   Kihei
Kahoolawe   Maui

H A W A I I

P A C I F I C   O C E A N

Hawi   Waimea
Kailua   Hilo
Captain Cook   Hawaii
Pahoa
Pahala
Naalehu

KEALIA POND NWR (Maui)—Hawaiian Coots, Hawaiian Stilts, Cattle Egrets, Black-crowned Night-Herons, and migrant shorebirds congregate at this 500-acre refuge. Contact: Kealia Pond NWR, P.O. Box 1042, Kihei, HI 96753; phone: 808-875-1582.

HAWAII VOLCANOES NATIONAL PARK Rainforest habitats in the higher elevations of this park are one of the best places to find Hawaiian honeycreepers. Watch for tropicbirds in the caldera of Kilauea Volcano. Contact Hawaii Volcanoes NP, P.O. Box 52, HI 96718-0052; 808-985-6000.

St. Paul Island Pribilof Islands (Alaska)—Enormous colonies of kittiwakes, murres, auklets, and puffins nest on St. Paul Island; Contact: TDX, 1500 West 33rd Avenue, Suite 220, Anchorage, AK 99503; phone: 907-278-1312.

Aleutian Islands (Alaska)—These are extremely remote seabird islands with enormous populations of puffins, fulmars, murres, kittiwakes, and others. Attu Island is famous for Siberian accidentals. Contact: Attour Air, 2027 Partridge Lane, Highland Park, IL 60035; phone: 1-888-BRD-ATTU.

Beaufort Sea

Barrow
Prudhoe Bay
Point Lay
Kaktovik
Kivalina
Colville River
Umiat
Weyok
Brooks Range
Fort Yukon
Deering
ALASKA
Wales
Fairbanks
Gambell
McKinley Park
Alakanuk
Alaska Range
Grayling
Gulkana
Susitna
Anchorage
Hope
Valdez
Katalla
Haines
Kwigillingok
Juneau
Platinum
Port Alexander
Kodiak
Gulf of Alaska
Ketchikan

RUSS FER.

Bering Strait

B e r i n g   S e a

Kuskokwim Mts.
Yukon River
Alaska Peninsula

A l e u t i a n   I s l a n d s
Belkofski
Atka
Dutch Harbor

P A C I F I C
O C E A N

Gulf of Alaska

Izembek NWR (Cold Bay, Alaska)—Black Brant, Lesser Canada Geese, Emperor Geese, and accompanying waterfowl were the prime reasons for managing this refuge, but the land also supports huge numbers of shorebirds, gyrfalcons, peregrines, Lapland Longspurs, Snow Buntings, and Arctic Terns. Contact: Izembek NWR, P.O. Box 127, 1 Izembek Drive, Cold Bay, AK 99571; phone: 907-532-2445.

Kenai National Moose Range (Kenai, Alaska)—This 3,000-square-mile refuge in southeast Alaska is home to much more than moose. Loons, Bald Eagles, Spruce Grouse, and Goshawks are common residents. Land birds, including Pine Grosbeaks, Golden-crowned Kinglets, and Varied Thrushes, nest at the refuge, and seabirds occur on several adjacent rocks. Contact: Kenai National Moose Range, Box 500, Kenai, AK 99611; phone: 907-283-4877.

APPENDIX I
BIRDER ETHICS

Everyone who enjoys birds and birding has an obligation to respect wildlife, habitat, and the rights of others. When a conflict of interest between birds and birders occurs, the welfare of the birds and their habitat must come first.

Code of Birding Ethics

1 Always consider your effect on birds and work to reduce disturbance.

Do not harass birds during observation, photography, sound recording, or filming.

Limit the use of recordings and other methods of attracting birds, and never use such methods in heavily birded areas, or for attracting any species that is locally, regionally, or nationally threatened or endangered.

Before advertising the presence of a rare bird, evaluate the potential for disturbance to the bird, its surroundings, and other people in the area, and proceed only if access can be controlled and disturbance minimized. The sites of rare nesting birds should be divulged only to the appropriate authorities.

Keep an appropriate distance from nests and nesting colonies so as not to disturb the birds or expose the nests to danger. Use a blind or hide for photography or extended nest observations.

Limit the use of artificial light for filming or photography, especially for close-ups.

Stay on roads, trails, and paths where they exist; otherwise minimize any habitat disturbance as much as possible.

2 Always respect the law and the rights of others. Respect "no trespassing" signs, and ask permission to enter private or posted lands.

Follow all laws, rules, and regulations governing use of public areas, both at home and abroad.

Practice common courtesy in contacts with landowners. Your exemplary behavior will generate goodwill with birders and non-birders alike.

Freely share your bird knowledge with others (except where code one applies). Wear your binoculars when entering coffee shops and stores when birding. Identifying yourself as a birder when you shop can help to show the economic benefit of birding.

3 Ensure that bird feeders, nest structures, and water supplies are safe.

Keep dispensers, water, and food clean and free of decay or disease. It's helpful to feed birds continuously during harsh weather.

Maintain and clean nest structures annually.

If you are attracting birds to an area, make sure that the birds are not exposed to predation from cats, dogs, and other domestic animals, or dangers posed by artificial hazards—especially windows.

4 Group birding, whether organized or impromptu, requires special care.

Group member responsibilities:

Help minimize disturbance to birds, the environment, and fellow birders.

If you witness unethical birding behavior, tell the person immediately and attempt, within reason, to stop it. If the behavior continues, document it, and inform others.

Respect the interests and skills of other birders. Be helpful to beginners.

Group Leader Responsibilities:

Assume responsibility for the conduct of the group.

Keep groups to a size that limits impact on the environment and does not interfere with others using the same area.

Make sure that everyone in the group knows of and practices this code. Teach through word and example.

Learn and inform the group of special circumstances applicable to the areas being visited (e.g., no tape recorders allowed).

Acknowledge that professional tour companies bear a special responsibility to place the welfare of birds and benefits of public knowledge ahead of the company's commercial interests. Ideally, leaders should keep track of tour sightings, document unusual occurrences, and submit records to appropriate organizations.

Adapted from the code published by the American Birding Association in its 1996 newsletter, Winging It.

APPENDIX II
BUILDING A BIRDER'S LIBRARY

The growing popularity of bird watching has created a flood of literature so great that it threatens to overwhelm the beginning bird enthusiast. For North America, there are dozens of books on identification, life histories, and bird finding. Each year new regional books appear, as well as new editions of college texts that attempt to keep pace with the burgeoning growth in ornithological research. While excellent books exist about most bird-watching topics, there are also many inferior titles that confuse the selection process.

This section offers recommendations for building a basic bird-watcher's library. This is not a review of all of the good choices available, but rather my recommendations for books and sound recordings that will prove most useful. When building your library of bird books, a useful goal would be to choose at least one entry from each of the following sections:

Field Guides

Compared to tropical countries, North America has relatively few birds—but unlike the tropics, North America has many excellent field guides. Any of the following guides can help you learn to identify birds.

National Geographic Society Field Guide to the Birds of North America, by Jon L. Dunn. 3rd ed. Washington, D.C.: The National Geographic Society, 1999; 480 pages. Contains color pictures, range maps, and descriptions of all North American breeding species, as well as many accidentals. With information and maps on the same page. Shows plumages for different sexes, ages, seasons, and color morphs. This expanded edition contains current common names.

A Field Guide to the Birds (Eastern) and *A Field Guide to Western Birds*, by Roger Tory Peterson. New York: Houghton Mifflin Co., 1980 (Eastern) and 1990 (Western); 384 and 432 pages. Still the best choice for beginners, these guides to bird identification include descriptions of each bird and its voice. Range maps have more details than other guides, but are in a separate section from color pictures. Arrows point to key field marks useful for identification.

A Field Guide to Birds' Nests Found East of the Mississippi and *A Field Guide to Western Birds' Nests*, by Hal H. Harrison. New York: Houghton Mifflin Co.,1975 (Eastern) and 1979 (Western); 257 and 279 pages. Contains detailed descriptions of the nests and eggs of nearly 300 species, including brief information on the breeding range and habitat, as well as special points of interest for each species. Also features color photographs of nests and eggs, and line drawings of adult birds, for most species.

Stokes Field Guide to Birds (Eastern or Western Region), by Donald and Lillian Stokes. Boston: Little,

Brown & Company, 1996; 472 and 520 pages. Illustrations are generally more useful for identification than photos, but this guide does a good job of providing multiple photos for many species, featuring color photographs of male, female, seasonal, and immature plumages, together with range map, species description, and conservation information. Also features colored tabs keyed to each bird group and special learning pages with helpful tips for challenging groups such as hawks in flight, shorebirds, and flycatchers.

Life Histories and General References

After identifying birds in the field, it's fun to do some reading at home. Make a point to read about the life histories of familiar birds and of new species as you see them. Knowledge of family life, migrations, and other features of behavior will add depth to your appreciation of birds.

The Audubon Society Encyclopedia of North American Birds, by John K. Terres. New York: Wings Books, 1991; 1109 pages. The most comprehensive and readable reference book written for both the general reader and the scientific community. Includes biographies of North American birds, bird biology, definitions of ornithological terms, and short biographies of famous ornithologists and naturalists; well illustrated with excellent color photos.

The Bird Almanac, by David M. Bird. Toronto: Key Porter Books Ltd, 1999; 512 pages. A complete list of world birds with conservation status, followed by lists of everything from flight speeds, egg shapes, body weights, longevity records, state birds, extreme records (e.g. highest flying, shortest tails, heaviest flying bird, etc.), Web sites, and more.

The Birder's Handbook, by Paul R. Ehrlich, David S. Dobkin, and Darryl Wheye. New York: Simon &

Schuster (Fireside), 1988; 785 pages. This excellent volume provides details about the nesting and feeding habits of each North American species, interspersed with short, general essays about avian behavior and natural history.

Birds of North America: Life Histories for the 21st Century. Nos. 1-360 as of August 1998. Published by the American Ornithologists Union and the Academy of Natural Sciences, 1992. Each issue is a separate, in-depth species account that includes information about habitat, behavior, ecology, plumage, body size, conservation and a review of available literature. Many accounts are in progress. Expensive to purchase, but available at many libraries.

A Guide to Bird Behavior, by Donald and Lillian Stokes. 3 vols. Boston: Little, Brown & Co., 1979, 1983, and 1989; 300-400 pages per volume. A different approach to birding through watching the behavior of common birds (25 species per volume), including detailed life history information, illustrated descriptions of displays, and suggestions on how to recognize songs and calls and their behavioral contexts.

Life Histories of North American Birds, by Arthur Cleveland Bent. 23 vols. New York: Dover Publications, 1963. Unabridged republication of this classic work (originally published by the United States National Museum) contains a wealth of information and anecdotes about breeding, food preferences, plumage, behavior, and migration. Includes information from author's own observations as well as those of many early naturalists. Note that names of some birds are different from current names. Available at many libraries.

Ornithology Textbooks

A college-level textbook will provide a resource capable of answering questions about such topics as anatomy, evolution, migration, senses, and flight;

either text suggested below will fill this important niche in your library.

The Life of Birds, by Joel C. Welty and Luis Baptista. Fort Worth, Texas: Harcourt College Publishers, 1988; 398 pages. This general textbook in basic ornithology is very readable, though a little out-of-date on a few topics. Contains an excellent index.

Ornithology, by Frank B. Gill. 2nd ed. New York: W. H. Freeman & Co., 1995; 766 pages. The most up-to-date general textbook in basic ornithology. Offers more scientific details though fewer examples than *The Life of Birds*. Useful appendix describes and illustrates major groups of birds of the world.

Attracting Birds

You can turn your backyard into a bird sanctuary by providing the right plants for food, protection, singing perches, and nesting sites. Landscaping for birds means arranging the plants in a useful way, while adding nest boxes and a water source. There are many mediocre books in this category, but here are a few especially helpful exceptions.

American Wildlife and Plants: A Guide to Wildlife Food Habits, by Alexander C. Martin, Herbert S. Zim, and Arnold L. Nelson. New York: Dover Publications, 1961; 500 pages. A guide to the trees, shrubs, weeds, and herbs used by birds and mammals of the United States. Treats wildlife by group (waterbirds, songbirds, etc.) and gives data on their foods (particularly plant parts), ranges, habits, and economics.

The Audubon Society Guide to Attracting Birds, by Stephen W. Kress. New York: Charles Scribner's Sons, 1985; 377 pages. Landscaping for birds, bird feeding, bird housing, and providing water; for large and small properties. Currently out of print, but available at many libraries.

The North American Bird Feeder Handbook, by Robert Burton. London: Dorling Kindersley, 1995;

225 pages. A National Audubon Society Book. Includes species profiles and excellent photos of the most common birds that visit feeders; feeder and nest box design.

The Bird Garden, by Stephen W. Kress. London: Dorling Kindersley, 1995; A National Audubon Society Book. 176 pages. Discusses many ways to attract birds to your backyard, from feeders and nest structures to ponds and gardens. Lists the plants that are most effective in attracting birds in different regions.

A Complete Guide to Bird Feeding, by John Dennis. New York: Alfred Knopf, 1994; 292 pages. Discusses different types of feeders, nontraditional foods to offer birds, and problems at feeders. Gives information on behavior, identification, and food preferences of feeder birds.

Landscaping for Wildlife, by Carrol L. Henderson. Minnesota Department of Natural Resources, 1987; 144 pages. A comprehensive guide to bringing wildlife to your yard or a larger piece of land; contains everything from landscape plans to tips on building brush piles, bird feeders, and frog ponds. Also contains detailed charts of plants and their use by wildlife. Available from MDNR: 117 University Avenue, St. Paul, MN, 55155.

Wild About Birds: The DNR Bird Feeding Guide, Minnesota Department of Natural Resources, 1995; 278 pages. Thorough guide to feeding birds; includes sections on specific birds and how to attract them, as well as sections focusing on different types of bird food, bird feeder types and how to build them, and troubleshooting. Available from MDNR (see above).

Woodworking for Wildlife by Carrol L. Henderson. Minnesota Department of Natural Resources, 1992; 111 pages. Detailed plans for constructing nest boxes, shelves, platforms, and roost boxes, plus information on how to locate and maintain the structures. Available from MDNR (see above).

Audio Guides

Birdsong recordings can help to confirm the voices that you hear in the field. Useful recordings of bird sounds should contain samples of songs and calls extensive enough to illustrate the varied nature of birdsongs and dialects.

Birding by Ear (Eastern/Central or Western Region), by Richard K. Walton and Robert W. Lawson. Peterson Field Guides. New York: Houghton Mifflin Co., 1989 and 1990. Three CDs or audio-cassettes and a booklet. The format of this popular guide works well for beginners as well as advanced birders. Covering 85 species east of the Rockies (or 91 species found west of the Great Plains), it groups birds with similar vocalizations and points out exactly what to listen for to tell them apart.

Know Your Bird Sounds, Vol. 1: Yard, Garden and City Birds; Vol. 2: Birds of the Countryside, by Lang Elliott. 1994. Published by NorthSound Music Group, Box 1360, Minocqua, WI 54548. Phone: 715-356-9800. Also available through One Good Tern, 1-800-432-8376. Sixty five-minute CD or audiocassette features songs and calls from 35 common species. Accompanying booklet gives detailed descriptions of the sounds of each bird, including the behavioral context for the calls. Good for beginners or those wanting to learn more than just songs.

More Birding by Ear: Eastern and Central and *Guide to Bird Sounds,* by the Cornell Laboratory of Ornithology and The National Geographic Society, 1994 and 1983. Two audiocassettes or CDs. Contain page number references to the National Geographic Society Field Guide to the Birds of North America. Includes calls, songs, and other sounds of 179 species.

Stokes Field Guide to Bird Songs, Eastern Region, and Western Region, by Lang Elliott with Donald and Lillian Stokes. Time-Warner Audio Books, 1999. CDs or audiocassettes and a booklet. Includes more species and different types of sounds than other guides to eastern birdsongs. The booklet has precise call and song descriptions for 552 species, including hints on distinguishing similar species.

Checklists

Checklists are a fun way to keep records of the birds you see. To track the birds you see, consider adding a North American and a world checklist. Names of North American birds are changed frequently to reflect advances in taxonomy. The American Ornithologists' Union's Checklist of North American Birds is considered the authoritative reference for bird names, and all of the birding checklists use it as a reference. Here are some recommendations.

ABA Checklist: Birds of the Continental United States and Canada. Austin, Tex. The American Birding Association, 1996. Now in its 5th edition, this is the official North American checklist of the American Birding Association. The ABA Checklist lists the 906 species recognized in the continental United States and Canada. Common names follow those used by the American Ornithologists' Union (AOU), but the list does not include the most recent changes presented in the AOU's, 7th edition of its checklist, published in 1998.

The AOU Checklist of North American Birds. The Committee on Classification and Nomenclature of the American Ornithologists' Union. 7th ed. Lawrence, Kan.: Allen Press, 1998; 829 pages. This authoritative reference provides common and scientific names, habitat, and distribution. It lists 2,008 species that occur north of Columbia, including the islands of the Caribbean and north to the date line in the Bering Sea between Russia and Alaska.

Birder's Journal. National Geographic Society, Washington, D.C., 1999; 480 pages. This book is a companion to the 3rd edition of the *National Geographic Society Field Guide to the Birds of North America.* This paperback follows the AOU's 1998 (7th ed.) list of North American birds and includes those known to occur in the continental U.S. and Canada. Each species has room for date, location, and several lines of notes opposite a page (reprinted from the field guide) that can be marked with further notes.

Birder's Life List & Diary. Edited by Steven C. Sibley. Ithaca, N.Y.: Cornell Laboratory of Ornithology, 1991; 212 pages. This spiral-bound book provides ample note-taking space for each of the 934 species found in North America north of Mexico, including Hawaii. It also includes distinct subspecies. The names follow the 1989 (6th ed.) of the AOU's *Check-list of North American Birds.*

Birds of the World: A Check List, by James F. Clements. Vista, Calif.: Ibis Publishing Co., 4th ed. 1991; 617pages. Annual supplements are available through 1997. For North America, includes name changes published by the AOU, but does not include changes published in the 1998 (7th ed.) of the AOU checklist. Provides space for date and location of first sighting and lists the general range of occurrence.

Bird Finding

Hundreds of state and local bird-finding books base their recommendations on the simple facts that birds associate with specific habitats and often return to the same locations from one year to the next. Check with the American Birding Association, local Audubon chapter, or booksellers that specialize in local references (see page 152) to find the best birding locations near your home.

The Birder's Guide to Bed and Breakfasts, by Peggy van Hulsteyn. 2nd ed. Santa Fe, N.Mex.: John Muir Publications, 1995; 401 pages. This guide is a wonderful companion to bird-finding guides as it provides birder-friendly accommodations at bed and breakfasts near many of North America's best birding locations.

Birdfinder: A Birder's Guide to Planning North American Trips, by Jerry A Cooper. Colorado Springs, Colo.: American Birding Association. 1995; 374 pages. Part of the ABA Bird Finding series, this spiral-bound field book provides information about nineteen short tours (each comprising a few days) of key birding areas within the United States (one in Canada). Daily suggestions are made in each tour. Provides detailed travel directions, phone numbers, birding hot lines, and places to stay.

Birdfinding in Forty National Forests and Grasslands. American Birding Association (ABA) and U.S. Forest Service. 1994; 192pages, This guide describes top birding routes in forty national forests and national grasslands in Alaska, the lower 48 states, and Puerto Rico. Available from ABA.

Finding Birds on US Bureau of Reclamation Lands. Edited by Alan Versaw. American Birding Association, 1999; 46 pages. The Bureau of Reclamation (BOR) units manage western riparian areas in seventeen western states, from the Dakotas south to Texas and west to the Pacific coast. This collaborative project between ABA and the U.S. Bureau of Reclamation provides information on twenty-two BOR properties. Available from ABA.

A Guide to Bird Finding East of the Mississippi, by Olin Sewall Pettingill, Jr. 2nd ed. New York: Oxford University Press, 1977; 689 pages, and *A Guide to Bird Finding West of the Mississippi,* by Olin Sewall Pettingill, Jr. 2nd ed. New York: Oxford University Press, 1981; 783pages. These thorough guides focus on national, state, and local parks and refuges that are likely to withstand development. Lists of characteristic species follow each habitat discussion. Lively accounts provide travel directions.

Guide to Birdwatching Sites, Eastern U.S., by Mel

White. Washington, D.C.: National Geographic Society, 1999; 320 pages, and *Guide to Birdwatching Sites, Western U.S.,* by Mel White. Washington, D.C.: National Geographic Society, 1999; 240 pages. Containing respectively more than 275 and 350 bird-finding sites in the eastern and western U.S., these convenient guides highlight many of the best sites for finding birds, providing maps, travel directions, local hot lines, contact phone numbers, all enhanced by National Geographic-style photography. These are current and valuable books for the traveling birder.

Guide to the National Wildlife Refuges, by William and Laura Riley. New York: Macmillan Publishing Co., 1993; 684 pages. This paperback guide provides detailed accounts of U.S National Wildlife Refuges, explaining which refuges are open to the public, how to get there, what to see and do, where visitors can stay or camp, the best times to visit, and much more. Easy-to-read state maps show the location of refuges in reference to nearby cities.

Regional Bird Books

Most states and provinces have one or more books describing birds to be found there as well as local checklists. Such books are very helpful for knowing which birds occur in your area, and when and where they occur. New books and lists appear daily, so the best approach is to contact a bookseller that specializes in bird books. The best source for regional books is the American Birding Association (ABA), P.O. Box 6599, Colorado Springs, CO, 80934, phone. 1-800-634-7736; e-mail: member@aba.org; for sales catalog call 1-800-634-7736, or e-mail: abasales @aba.org; Web site: http:\\www.americanbirding.org

ORGANIZATIONS AND PERIODICALS

Bird Magazines

Bird magazines provide popular articles about topics such as birding locations, bird biology, and conservation issues. They also provide timely announcements of coming events and new birding products. There are many excellent magazines available; here are a few choices.

Bird Conservation, American Bird Conservancy, 1250 24th Street, NW, Suite 400, Washington, DC 20037. The magazine of Partners in Flight, the cooperative agency and nonprofit group of organizations concerned with bird conservation. Features timely articles about conservation concerns and successes in both North and South America.

Bird Watcher's Digest, P.O. Box 110, Marietta, OH 45750. Bimonthly, digest-sized magazine aimed at a broad cross section of the bird-watching public. Lively articles are often personal and anecdotal in style, but all aspects of avian natural history are regularly featured. Also includes regular columns and short bird news items.

Birder's World, 44 East 8th Street, Suite 410, Holland, MI 49423. Handsome, bimonthly, glossy magazine featuring fine color photography and entertaining and informative full-length articles and photo essays on all aspects of birds and birding. Each issue contains in-depth species accounts, a featured birding hot spot, regular columns, shorter bird news items, and a gallery of bird photographs taken by readers.

Birding, American Birding Association (ABA), P.O. Box 6599, Colorado Springs, CO 80934. Bimonthly magazine of the American Birding Association. Articles usually slanted toward the technical aspects of birding, helping develop readers' identification skills. Promotes recreational birding and fosters public appreciation of birds and their importance in the environment. Illustrated with color photographs.

Living Bird, Cornell Laboratory of Ornithology, 159 Sapsucker Woods Road, Ithaca, NY 14850. Elegant, quarterly color magazine for members. Designed to appeal to bird enthusiasts ranging from amateur bird-watchers to professional ornithologists. Features authoritative, thought-provoking, and timely articles, often by leading ornithologists, on all aspects of birding, bird biology, and conservation. A showcase for the finest bird photography, often featuring portfolios and large spreads.

WildBird, P.O. Box 52898, Boulder, CO 80322. Colorful monthly magazine with lively style and layout. Articles emphasize the fun and excitement of birding in the field, featuring both national and international hot spots. Also includes species profiles, regular columns, and an annual bird photography contest open to readers.

Ornithology Journals

Scientific journals are not very useful for beginning birders, but serious amateurs should subscribe to at least one of the professional journals to better follow developments in the field of ornithology. Abstracts from journals may be found at Web sites.

The Auk, American Ornithologists' Union, c/o Division of Birds MRC 116, National Museum of Natural History, Washington, DC 20560. Features full-length articles on original research findings in bird biology in the broadest sense, from laboratory, field, and museum studies. Studies may be experimental or descriptive, but information is generally interpreted within a conceptual context. Also presents review articles and short communications. Web site: pica.wru.umt.edu/AOU/AOU.htm

The Condor, Cooper Ornithological Society, 810 East 10th Street, Lawrence, KS 66044. Features full-length experimental or descriptive, often conceptually based, articles on original research findings in many aspects of the biology of wild birds. Oriented more toward field studies than *The Auk.* Historically has had a western U.S. focus, but now international in scope. Also presents short communications and occasional review articles. Web site: www.cooper.org

The Journal of Field Ornithology, Association of Field Ornithologists, 810 East 10th Street, Lawrence, KS 66044. Features articles emphasizing both life history descriptions and experimental studies of wild birds in the field, as well as field methodology, including conservation techniques. Biased toward studies from the western hemisphere. Strong interest in field studies in the neotropics and those involving amateur participation. Web site: www.afonet.org

The Wilson Bulletin, Wilson Ornithological Society, the Josselyn Van Tyne Memorial Library, Museum of Zoology, University of Michigan, Ann Arbor, MI 48109-1079. Features full-length articles on original research findings in many aspects of bird biology and short communications describing observations of particular interest. Content and style make it accessible to both amateur and professional ornithologists. Web site: www.ummz.lsa.umich.edu/birds/wos.html

Organizations

There are many local, state, provincial, and national organizations concerned with bird watching and conservation of specific groups. The following are some of the national groups concerned with birds and their conservation, most of which publish newsletters and magazines. For a more complete listing of bird organizations see *Conservation Directory,* an annual publication of the National Wildlife Federation, 8925 Leesburg Pike Vienna, VA 22184-0001 and *The Bird Almanac,* by David M. Bird, available from: Key Porter Book, 70 The Esplanade, Toronto, ON Canada M5E 1R2.

Canada

Bird Studies Canada, P.O. Box 160, Port Rowan, ON NOE 1MO; phone: 519-586-3531

British Columbia Field Ornithologists, P.O. Box 8059, Victoria, BC, Canada V8W 3R7; phone: 250-744-2521

Ducks Unlimited Canada, 1190 Waverley Street, Winnipeg, MB R3T 2E2; phone: 204-477-1760

Nova Scotia Bird Society, Nova Scotia Museum of Natural History, 1747 Summer Street, Halifax, NS B3H 3A6; phone: 902-429-4610

Ontario Field Ornithologists, Box 62014, Burlington Mall Postal Outlet, Burlington, ON L7R 4K2

Partners in Flight-Canada, P.O. Box 79040, Hull, PQ J8Y 6V2

The Province of Quebec Society for the Protection of Birds, P.O. Box 43, Station B, Montreal, PQ H3B 3J5; phone: 514-637-2141

United States

American Bird Conservancy,1250 24th Street NW, Suite 400,Washington, DC 20037; phone: 202-778-9666; Web site: www.abcbirds.org

American Birding Association, P.O. Box 6599, Colorado Springs, CO 80934; phone: 719-578-1480; Web site: www.americanbirding.org

Birdlife International (U.S. Office), c/o World Wildlife Fund, 1250 24th Street, NW, Washington, DC 20037; phone:202-778-9563

The Cornell Laboratory of Ornithology, 159 Sapsucker Woods Road, Ithaca, NY 14850; phone: 607-254-2473; Web site: birds.cornell.edu

Ducks Unlimited, Inc, One Waterfowl Way, Long Grove, IL 60047; phone: 708-438-4300

Hawk Migration Association of North America, Box 3482, Lynchburg, VA 24503; phone: 804-847-7811

Hawk Mountain Sanctuary Association, RD 2, Box 191, Kempton, PA 19529-6961; phone: 610-756-6961

National Audubon Society, 700 Broadway, New York, NY 10003-9501; phone: 212-979-3000; Web site: www.audubon.org

National Fish and Wildlife Foundation, 1120 Connecticut Avenue, NW, Suite 900, Washington, DC 20036; Web site: www.nfwf.org

Pacific Seabird Group, Oregon Institute of Marine Biology, University of Oregon, P.O. Box 5389, Charleston, OR 97420; Web site: www.nmnh.si.edu/BIRDNET/PacBirds/

Partners in Flight, US Fish and Wildlife Service, Office of Migratory Bird Management, 4401 N. Fairfax Drive, Room 634, Arlington, VA 22203; Web site: www.pif.nbs.gov/pif

Purple Martin Conservation Association, Edinboro University of Pennsylvania, Edinboro, PA 16444; phone: 814-734-4420

Roger Tory Peterson Institute, 110 Marvin Parkway, Jamestown, NY 14701; phone: 716-665-BIRD

Smithsonian Migratory Bird Center, National Zoo, Washington, DC 20008; phone: 202-673-4908; Web site: www.si.edu/natzoo/zooview/smbc/smbchome.htm

Waterbird Society c/o National Museum of Natural History, Smithsonian Institute, Washington, DC 20560; Web site: www.nmnh.si.edu/BIRDNET/CWS/

APPENDIX IV

BIRDING IN CYBERSPACE

The Internet provides enormous possibilities for birders and for bird conservation, providing instant information about birding locations, bird sightings and even sharing the living contents within bird nests! Scientists are especially excited about using the Internet to link amateur birders to provide real-time data collection about everything from birds at feeders to warbler counts and nest box monitoring. There are already hundreds of sites devoted to birds, and unfortunately they cannot all be listed here. The following are some of the best gateways to birding on the World Wide Web.

Birder: http://birder.com/index.html Primarily oriented to amateurs, with information about birds, birding techniques, and birding locations. Includes extensive checklists (national and global), birding hot spots, rare bird alert telephone numbers and transcripts, birding guides listed geographically, and backyard birding tips. A scientific section has links to ornithological societies, museum collections, and taxonomic information. A fun-and-games section features bird quizzes, photos and sound, and news of upcoming birding festivals and conferences.

Bird Monitoring: www.im.nbs.gov/birds.html This Web site provides links to many bird monitoring programs administered by governmental and nongovernmental organizations throughout the United States and Canada. Many of these programs provide access to bird population data and information about how to become a participant. The following are some examples. The Canadian Bird Checklist Program allows bird observations to be contributed on-line. The Audubon Christmas Bird Count provides bird distribution maps and other

information summaries, describes how the data were collected, and suggests potential applications. The North American Bird Banding Program describes why and how bird banding data are used and how to report a recovered bird band. The North American Breeding Bird Survey provides a continent-wide perspective on bird population changes, from summarized data collected annually since 1966.

BirdNet: http://www.nmnh.si.edu/BIRDNET/index.html This site is a service of the Ornithological Council, a public information organization involving eight North American professional ornithological societies. Primarily oriented to the scientific study of birds. Extensive links to research news; professional information including graduate programs in ornithology, research funding sources, and careers in ornithology; and links to biologists on-line.

BirdSource: http://birdsource.cornell.edu An interactive site cosponsored by the Cornell Laboratory of Ornithology (CLO) and the National Audubon Society, this partnership between birders and scientists has created a powerful tool for bird conservation. Birders contribute their birding observations on-line, and the data are analyzed by CLO and Audubon Society staff, helping to define bird ranges, breeding distributions, migratory pathways, and habitat needs. Projects currently include the Winter Finch Survey and Warbler Watch, which tracks the migration and breeding distribution of North American warblers.

Cornell Laboratory of Ornithology: http://birds.cornell.edu This Web site provides information about the laboratory's many research and education programs. Visitors can access information, including maps, graphs, and tables of research results, on the lab's various citizen-science projects, such as Project FeederWatch, Classroom BirdWatch, and the Cornell Nest Box Network. This site also provides information on the lab's Library of Natural Sounds and photographic slide collection, through which animal sounds and bird slides can be purchased.

Electronic Resources on Ornithology: http://www.chebucto.ns.ca/Environment/NHR/ bird.html This Web site provides links to a huge variety of bird-related Web sites around the world, including birding and ornithological organizations (local, regional, national, and international), museums, research centers, conservation programs, commercial Web sites (for example, birding software and book publishers), and birding chat groups.

Ornithological Bibliographies: http://aves.net/the-owl/blnkbibl.htm This Web site is an exhaustive bibliography of ornithological literature, on-line magazines, and discussion groups.

APPENDIX V

EDUCATION PROGRAMS

Education programs can provide beginning bird enthusiasts with new and rewarding experiences while promoting a greater understanding and appreciation of birds. The educational programs that follow are divided into two principal groups: field courses and internships, and curricula and activities manuals about birds. Check with your local nature center or college to find a birding or ornithology course near you. International bird tours are advertised in popular birding magazines such as *Birding* and *Birder's World*, listed in appendix III.

Field Courses and Internships

Atlantic Center Intern Program— Atlantic Center for the Environment, 951 Highland Street, Ipswich, MA 01938. Web site: http://www.qlf.org The Center provides year-round internships and summer staff positions concerning bird-related projects. Projects include conducting bird education programs in schools, seabird inventories, and gannet restoration. Most project sites are in northern Maine or one of the Atlantic provinces. Participants must be 21 years old and have some experience in ornithology or related natural sciences.

Audubon Camps— National Audubon Society, 700 Broadway, New York, NY 10003-9501. Web site: http://www.Audubon.org The Audubon Camps offer resident summer courses for adults interested in the natural environment. Each of the three camps is a completely equipped learning center with dormitories, dining hall, and laboratory facilities. The camps are located in coastal Maine, rural Connecticut, and the mountains of Wyoming. All

offer natural history courses for beginning students that interpret birds as part of their ecosystem.

Great Gull Island— Department of Ornithology, American Museum of Natural History, Central Park West at 79th Street, New York, NY 10024. Web site: http://wso.williams.edu/~wchang/terns/Terns.html The American Museum of Natural History conducts long-term studies of Common and Roseate Terns on Great Gull Island, located at the eastern end of Long Island Sound. During the spring-summer breeding season, volunteers help professionals band and monitor nesting terns. Participants must be prepared for long hours and primitive living conditions. Inquiries about summer volunteer positions should be submitted by January or February, prior to the breeding season.

The Library of Natural Sounds— Laboratory of Ornithology, Cornell University, 159 Sapsucker Woods Road, Ithaca, NY 14850. Web site: http://birds.cornell.edu/LNS Field recording classes and teams of participants are sometimes organized to explore a selected locality and record the sounds of birds and other animals. Participants help subsidize costs and do most of the data gathering and recording. The Library of Natural Sounds welcomes contributing recordists. The library provides information, advice, technical assistance, and tape to persons willing to record for the collection. Recordings from the library are available to anyone with an interest in animal sounds.

Long Point Bird Observatory— P.O. Box 160, Port Rowan, ON N0E 1M0, Canada. Web site: http://www.mb.ec.gc.ca/ENGLISH/LIFE/WHP/gfb_vlist.html The observatory conducts a year-round program at its headquarters on the shore of Lake Erie and an April-October operation of isolated field stations on Long Point that are staffed by volunteers under the direction of professionals. Activities include Project FeederWatch, loon monitoring, banding, and educational programs. Internships and volunteer opportunities are available.

Manomet Center for Conservation Sciences— Box 936, Manomet, MA 02345. Web site: http//jasper.stanford.edu/OBFS/OBFS_Stations/MA_Manomet_Bird_Observ._html Interns work with staff biologists concerning ongoing field research programs for two months or longer and have the opportunity to develop independent research projects. Training is also offered to licensed banders and volunteers interested in updating or learning bird-banding skills.

Point Reyes Research Volunteer Program— Point Reyes Bird Observatory, 4990 Shoreline Highway, Stinson Beach, CA 94970. Web site: http://www.igc.apc.org/prbo/ Volunteers usually spend three months at the Palomarin Field Station, located at the Point Reyes National Seashore. Participants study the population dynamics of resident land birds, monitor the coastal land bird migration, map breeding territories, and band birds. Opportunities are also available for volunteers to assist seabird studies on the Farallon Islands. Qualified applicants should have prior experience with bird research.

Bird Curricula and Activity Manuals

The following references are for programs with national or regional value, but there are many more choices available from the ABA (see page 152).

The Arctic Nesting Shorebirds Curriculum— For grades K-12, this curriculum provides activities, field trip plans, cultural exchange ideas, and background information for teachers on shorebird ecology, migration, and wetland ecosystems. The curriculum includes the Fish and Wildlife Service's Shorebird Sister Schools Program, an on-line Internet education program in which students can chat with each other and ask biologists questions about shorebirds and migration. Available from: Circumpolar Press, Box 221955, Anchorage, AK 99522; phone: 907-242-6416.

Birds Beyond Borders— This international program links children in the western U.S. with students in Mexico in the study of migratory songbirds. Activities were produced by teachers in both countries. The program includes classroom and field activities, pen pals between classrooms, and a teacher exchange in which teachers visit each other's classrooms. Available from: Colorado Bird Observatory, 13401 Piccadilly Road, Brighton, CO 80601; phone: 303-659-4348.

Birds, Birds, Birds— This issue of *Naturescope* is a rich collection of information and activities for grades K-8. There are five chapters covering topics of bird biology and conservation. The paperback booklet contains activities and pages that can be duplicated for classroom distribution. Available from: National Wildlife Federation, 8925 Leesburg Pike, Vienna, VA 22184; phone: 1-800-822-9919.

Bring Back the Birds— This is a collection of activities and conservation projects concerned with songbird decline and conservation, for grades 6-12.

It provides sound ecology background and suggests both quick activities that may be completed in an hour and land conservation projects that could span decades. Conservation International- Canada, 1415 Bathurst Street, Suite 202, Toronto, ON M5R 3H8 Canada; phone: 416-535-3052.

Classroom Feederwatch—Elementary-school children identify and count birds that visit their feeders and use the Internet to share data with scientists; analyze data to answer their own questions; use their findings to describe how the natural world works; and publish results in Classroom Birdscope, a newsletter written and designed by students. Contact: Cornell Laboratory of Ornithology, P.O. Box 11, Ithaca, NY 14851-0011; phone: 607-254-2427.

Hawk Mountain Sanctuary Pre-Visit Teacher's Packet— This is a packet of information designed for classes visiting this world-renowned hawk migration location in Pennsylvania, but the lessons, activities, and background material are suitable for anyone interested in teaching children (grades 3-6) about hawks. The materials include information about fall migration and nesting habits. Available from: Hawk Mountain Sanctuary, RR2, Box 191, Kempton, PA 19529-9449; phone: 610-756-6961.

Hunters of the Sky— Focused on raptors, this booklet is an excellent source of background information and activities about birds of prey for grades 4-10. Sections include topics on feathers, senses, and other raptor adaptations as well as activities. Available from: Science Museum of Minnesota, 30 East 10th Street, Saint Paul, MN 55101; phone: 612-221-4543.

Journey North: A Distance-Learning Adventure— This Internet-based program is available from February to June, providing "live" updates daily for over a dozen species including eagles, loons, songbirds, whales, and monarch butterflies. Satellite telemetry helps track some migrations, and there is a link to scientists who study migration. For grades 4-12. Available from: Journey North, 18150 Breezy Point Road, Wayzata, MN 55391; phone: 612-476-6470.

Project PigeonWatch—This research project focuses inner-city students (grades 4-12) on data collection about pigeon behavior and encourages consideration of why pigeons have such variable color patterns. Available from: Cornell Laboratory of Ornithology, PPW, P.O. Box 11, Ithaca, NY 14851-0011; phone: 607-254-2440.

Project Puffin and Giving Back to the Earth— This award-winning book and activity manual present an account of the restoration of Atlantic Puffins to Eastern Egg Rock, Maine, with abundant hands-on activities about seabird adaptations and conservation. Available from: Tilbury House, 132 Water Street, Gardiner, ME 04345; phone: 1-800-582-1899.

Save our Migratory Songbirds— This collaborative effort of researchers in the U.S., Canada, Argentina, and Mexico provides international perspectives about migration. The program links students across borders as pen pals. For grades 6-8. Available from: Manomet Center for Conservation Sciences, P.O. Box 1770, Manomet, MA 02345; phone: 508-224-6521.

Seminars in Ornithology: A Home Study Course in Bird Biology— Seminars in Ornithology is a home-study, college-level, noncredit course in ornithology. Completely revised in a new 1999 edition, each of ten chapters contains authoritative text by leading ornithologists about such topics as behavior, migration, and flight. The course includes a wealth of diagrams, maps, charts, photographs, and drawings. Students complete question sheets at the conclusion of each seminar that are checked by an instructor. Contact: Seminars in Ornithology, 159 Sapsucker Woods Road, Ithaca, NY 14850; phone: 607-254-BIRD. Web site: http://www.ornith.cornell.edu/homestudy/index.html

RESEARCH PROGRAMS WELCOMING AMATEURS

The science of ornithology is fortunate to have a high proportion of amateur participants. Organizers of an increasing number of bird research programs recognize the growing number of willing amateur participants and welcome their assistance. Most of North America's most effective bird monitoring studies are dependent on large numbers of volunteers. Benefits are derived from both directions. Professional ornithologists receive enthusiastic and often skilled assistance, and amateur birders learn more about bird biology and find satisfaction from assisting researchers.

The ranks of amateur ornithologists include a high proportion of professionals who offer a wide assortment of valuable experience and skills. Organizers of research programs should recognize that most amateurs watch birds during their leisure time for relaxation and recreation; the most successful cooperative programs are those that retain the "fun" element of bird watching.

Bird counts, censuses, and surveys are the most frequent "employers" of amateur participants. Without such input, most large-scale population monitoring and distribution studies would not generate enough field data to reveal continent-wide or local trends. Likewise, studies of bird behavior such as Cornell University's Nest Box Network are able to ask and answer questions about nesting ecology at a national level that can have great benefit for the management of cavity nesting birds. After analyzing data from across the country, scientists are able to recommend specific nestbox management techniques such as when to clean boxes or provide feathers or calcium supplements. Involving the public in data collection has become so widespread that it is often called "citizen science." The ultimate benefit is that a public engaged in meaningful observation and data collection will become more caring, serve as more effective stewards, and ultimately work for bird conservation.

Professional ornithologists seeking student research assistants for paid internships and volunteers often post projects in the Ornithological Newsletter On-Line, a publication of the Ornithological Societies of North America (OSNA) (http://www.ornith.cornell.edu/OSNA/ornnewsl.htm) Also visit OSNA at http://www.nmnh.si.edu/BIRDNET/OSNA/ or join one of the OSNA societies (American Ornithologists' Union, Association of Field Ornithologists, Waterbird Society, Cooper Ornithological Society, Raptor Research Foundation, and Wilson Ornithological Society) which entitle members to receive the OSNA newsletter. For membership, write OSNA, P.O. Box 1897, Lawrence, KS 66044-8897.

Opportunities for birders to assist research programs are so numerous that the American Birding Association (in cooperation with many federal agencies) compiles an annual booklet with 650 projects, mostly in North America. To obtain the most recent copy of "Opportunities for Birders," write to American Birding Association, P.O. Box 6599, Colorado Springs, CO 80934-6599, or call 719-578-9703. The complete directory is also accessible at the ABA Web site: www.americanbirding.org

National Programs Welcoming Amateur Birders

Birds in Forested Landscapes: This study focuses on the relationships between habitat characteristics and presence and the nesting success of seven North American thrush species and Sharp-shinned and Cooper's hawks. The goal of the program is to develop management prescriptions for these thrushes and hawks, which share dependence on forest interior habitat. Data are needed throughout the forests of North America during the nesting season (March-July), depending on the location of study areas. Participants must visit each site at least two times. Contact: Birds in Forested Landscapes, Cornell Laboratory of Ornithology, 159 Sapsucker Woods Road, Ithaca, NY 14850; phone: 607-254-BIRD; Web site:http:\\birds.cornell.edu

Breeding Bird Survey: Sponsored by the U.S. Fish and Wildlife Service and the Canadian Wildlife Service, the Breeding Bird Survey (BBS) is the principal tool for determining the status of North American breeding bird populations. Each June, volunteer observers drive over

4,100 BBS routes across the continental U.S. and Canada. Each route is 24.5 miles long and consists of fifty three-minute point counts of birds spaced at half-mile intervals on secondary roads. Observers need to be able to identify birds by sight and sound. In the U.S., contact: Breeding Bird Survey, USGS Patuxent Wildlife Research Center, 12100 Beech Forest Road, Laurel, MD 20708-4038; phone: 301-497-5843; Web site: http://www.mp2-pwrc.usgs.gov/bbs/bbsops.html; in Canada contact: BBS, Canadian Wildlife Service, National Wildlife Research Centre, Hull, PQ K1A 0H3; phone: 819-953-1425.

Christmas Bird Count: The Christmas Bird Count is the longest-running monitoring scheme in the world. Since 1900, bird enthusiasts have tallied winter birds and compiled their findings for an overview of bird populations. Now more than 30,000 participants annually assist this count, tallying more than 120 million birds. All historical data from Christmas Day of 1900 to the present are entered into a relational database in BirdSource (see Appendix IV) and are available for perusal by compilers, CBC participants, researchers, and other bird enthusiasts. Contact: National Audubon Society, 700 Broadway, New York, NY 10003; phone: 212-979-3000. Also see the BirdSource Web site: http://birdsource.cornell.edu/cbc/index.html

Earthwatch Institute: Earthwatch volunteers work with professional ornithologists on projects around the world to study and protect wild birds. Teams of participants spend two to three weeks in the field, where they learn research skills such as bird banding and bird behavior monitoring. Earthwatch is open to adults of all ages and occupations. Participants share the costs of the expedition. Contact: Earthwatch Institute, 10 Juniper Road, Box 127K, Belmont, MA 02178; phone: 1-800-776-0188; Web site: www.earthwatch.org

Important Bird Areas: The goal of this program is to identify, catalogue, and conserve significant bird habitats within each state. Volunteers nominate locations based on standard criteria. The selected sites are then prioritized for conservation. Important Bird Areas is part of the Partners in Flight Bird Conservation Plan. To obtain nomination forms, contact: IBA National Coordinator, National Audubon Society, Miles Wildlife Sanctuary, 99 West Cornwall Road, Sharon CT 06069; phone: 860-364-0048.

International Shorebird Surveys: Volunteers identify and count shorebirds at key locations three times a month during migration periods. The goal of the program is to learn which shorebirds concentrate at migration staging sites to learn which areas are especially important to shorebirds and to evaluate changes in shorebird populations. Contact: ISS, Manomet Center for Conservation Sciences, Manomet, MA 02345.

Migration Monitoring (Hawkwatching): This Canadian-based program provides population trends for daytime migrating raptors by counting birds at key migration locations. Observers should be able to recognize hawks at a distance (training is provided), to tally the hawks by species per hour, and to record weather details. Hawks are counted at the following locations:
Niagara Peninsula Hawkwatch: Glenn Barnett, 87 Highland Park Drive, Dundas, ON L9H 6G5.
High Park, Toronto and vicinity: John Barker, 4101 Westminster Place, Unit 55, Mississauga, ON L4W 4X4.
Hawk Cliff: Sue Ross, 483 George Street, Port Stanley, ON N5L 1H1.
Calgary: Wayne Smith, Hawk Watching, Calgary, AB; phone: 403-932-5183.
Bruce Peninsula: Mark Wiercinski, R.R. #4, Wiarton, ON N0H 2T0; phone: 519-534-3004.

Monitoring Avian Productivity and Survivorship (MAPS) Program: Land bird monitoring programs at specific locations in California, Indiana, Kansas, Kentucky, Maryland,

Massachusetts, Missouri, North Carolina, Oregon, Texas, Virginia, and the state of Washington. Volunteers with advanced experience assist bird banders and assist with vegetation descriptions conducted during ten-day intervals at each station. Interns are provided with housing and a per diem and travel reimbursement. Contact: The Institute for Bird Populations, P.O. Box 1346, Point Reyes Station, CA 94956; phone: 415-663-1436.

The Nest Box Network: This continent-wide study concerns the conservation of cavity-nesting birds such as bluebirds, tree swallows, chickadees, and many others. Participants collect data related to several research questions. Activities include counting the eggs in nest boxes, offering feathers to swallows for their nests, estimating the number of feathers in swallow nests, offering calcium, and much more. Participants learn how and where to put up nest boxes and how to check boxes without harming the birds. Participants pay an annual fee to participate and can submit data through the Internet or on paper forms. Contact: The Cornell Nest Box Network, Cornell Laboratory of Ornithology, 159 Sapsucker Woods Road, Ithaca, NY 14850; Phone: (607)254-BIRD; Web site: http:\\birds.cornell.edu

Nest Record Schemes: This program determines breeding success, distribution, and habitat use of Canadian birds. Participants record data from nests, including species, date, number of eggs or young, location, habitat, nest description, and nest fate. Participants complete standard data cards and return these to a regional coordinator. There are five centers for the collection of nesting information in Canada. British Columbia: Wayne Campbell, Ministry of Environment, Lands and Parks, 4th Floor, 2975 Jutland Road, Victoria, BC V8T 9M1; phone: 250-356-1376. Prairie Region: Herb Copland, Manitoba Museum of Man and Nature, 190 Rupert Avenue, Winnipeg, MB R3B 0N2. Maritimes: George Peck, Royal Ontario Museum,

100 Queen's Park Cr., Toronto, ON M5S 2C6. Quebec: Michel Gosselin, Canadian Museum of Nature, Box 3443, Station D, Ottawa, ON K1P 6P4; phone: (613)566-4291.

Yukon: The Yukon Bird Club, Box 31054, Whitehorse, Yukon, Y1A 5P7.

Prairie Shorebird Survey: Identify important lakes and wetlands used by Arctic breeding shorebirds during migration for staging and resting areas in the prairie provinces of Canada— Alberta, Saskatchewan, and Manitoba. Participants count shorebirds and provide information on species and numbers of shorebirds during daily counts from April through October. Contact: Canadian Wildlife Service, room 200, 4999 98th Avenue, Edmonton, AB T6B 2X3; phone: 403 951-0670.

Project FeederWatch: Anyone with a bird feeder can participate in this well-established citizen-science program of the Cornell Laboratory of Ornithology, National Audubon Society, Bird Studies Canada, and the Canadian Nature Federation. Feeder watchers count the highest numbers of each species they see at their feeders from November through April. The data are sent back to Cornell either through BirdSource (Appendix IV) or by paper forms. The data are used to show the size and distribution of winter birds that visit feeders. Participants pay a fee and receive the newsletter Birdscope. In the U.S., contact: Project FeederWatch, Cornell Laboratory of Ornithology, 159 Sapsucker Woods Road, Ithaca, NY 14850; 800-843-2473. In Canada, Project FeederWatch, Bird Studies Canada, P.O. Box 160, Port Rowan, ON, N0E 1M0; phone: 519-586-3531; Web site: http:\\birdsource.cornell.edu

Project PigeonWatch: Rock Doves are ideal study subjects for this international survey of pigeon flock coloration and behavior. This is an ideal program for urban youth, leaders, and teachers. Urban citizen scientists gather data on pigeons and send it to the Cornell Laboratory of Ornithology. The study uses field observations to understand why wild pigeons continue to have so many colors. Participants (or sponsors) pay a fee and receive a research packet that includes a booklet, data forms, and a pigeon poster with activities. Contact: Project PigeonWatch, Cornell Laboratory of Ornithology, 159 Sapsucker Woods Road, Ithaca, NY 14850; phone: 607-254-2403; Web site: http:\\birds.cornell.edu

Student Conservation Association: A wide range of projects for college-age students run for twelve to sixteen weeks. Conservation associate positions run six to twelve months. Projects include identifying, surveying, and researching birds as well as participating in public education about birds. Techniques learned include monitoring endangered species, mist-netting, banding, and analyzing data. Contact: SCA, P.O. Box 550, Charlestown, NH 03603; phone: 603-543-1700; Web site: www.sca-inc.org

Bird Research Centers

Cape May Bird Observatory, New Jersey Audubon Society, Box 3, Cape May Point, NJ 08212; Web site: www.nj.com/audubon/abtnjas/cmbo.html

Cornell Laboratory of Ornithology, 159 Sapsucker Woods Road, Ithaca, NY 14850; phone: 607-254-BIRD; Web site: http:\\birds.cornell.edu

Institute for Field Ornithology, University of Maine at Machias, 9 O'Brien Avenue, Machias, ME 04654; phone: 207-255-3313; Web site: http:\\www.umm.maine.edu/ifo/

Long Point Bird Observatory, Box 160, Port Rowan, ON, N0E 1M0; Web site: http:\\www.bsc-eoc.org/bscmain.html

Manomet Center for Conservation Sciences, P.O. Box 936, Manomet, MA 02345, 508/224-6521; Web site: http:www.manomet.org/

Point Reyes Bird Observatory, 4990 State Route, Stinson Beach, CA 94970; Web site: http:\\www.igc.apc.org/prbo/

APPENDIX VII
SOURCES FOR SUPPLIES

Optical Equipment

Bogen Photo Corp., 565 E. Crescent Avenue, P.O. Box 506, Ramsey, NJ 07446-0506; phone: 201-818-9500; Web site: http://www.bogenphoto.com/

Bushnell Sports Optics Worldwide, 9200 Cody Street, Overland Park, KS 66214; phone: 1-800-423-3537

Canon USA, Inc.; One Canon Plaza, Lake Success, NY 11042; phone: 516-488-6700

Carl Zeiss Optical, 1015 Commerce Street, Petersburg, VA 23803; phone: 1-800-338-2984

Leica Camera Inc., 156 Ludlow Avenue, Northvale, NJ 07647; phone: 201-767-8666; Web site: http://www.leica-camera-usa.com

Nikon Inc., 1300 Walt Whitman Road, Melville, NY 11747; phone: 516-547-4200; Web site: http://www.nikonusa.com/index.html

Questar Corporation, P.O. Box 59, New Hope, PA 18938; phone: 215-862-5277

Swarovski Optik North America Ltd., One Wholesale Way, Cranston, RI 02920; phone: 1-800-426-3089

Vivitar Corp., 1280 Rancho Conejo Boulevard, Newbury Park, CA 91320; phone: 1-800-498-7008

Birding Book Sources

Amazon.com http://www.amazon.com

American Birding Association (ABA), P.O. Box 6599, Colorado Springs, CO 80934; phone: 1-800-634-7736; e-mail: member@aba.org; sales catalog: 1-800-634-7736, or e-mail: abasales@aba..org Web site: www.americanbirding.org

The Aviary Bookstore, 111 Pullen Road.,
Rockwall, TX 75087, phone: 972-771-7965; Web site: theaviary.com

Barnes and Noble Booksellers, Web site: http://www.BarnesandNoble

Buteo Books, P.O. Box 425, Friday Harbour, WA 98250, phone: 1-800-722-2460 (orders); 1-804-263-8671.

Los Angeles Audubon Society Bookstore, 7377 Santa Monica Boulevard, Los Angeles, CA, 90046; phone: 213-876-0202; Web site: http://pw1.netcom.com

Massachusetts Audubon Society Bookstore, Great Road, Lincoln, MA 01773; 617-259-9807; Web site: http://www.massaudubon.org

Bird Feeders and Accessories

Aspects, Inc. Web site: Birdfeeding.com

BirdWatcher's Marketplace, 3150 Plainfield Avenue NE, Grand Rapids, MI 49525; phone: 616-365-1872 or 1-800-981-BIRD; Web site: birdwatchers.com

Cornell Laboratory Birding Shop. Web site: birds.cornell.edu

Wild Bird General Store, 4712 - 99 Street, Edmonton, AB T6E 5H5; phone: 403-439-7333, 1-800-465-5099; Web site: www.freenet.edmonton.ab.ca/wildbird/

Wildbird Emporium, 21 Olde Towne Road, Auburn, NH 03032; phone: 603-483-5523; Web site: www.wbird.com/

Wild Birds Unlimited, Cornell Laboratory of Ornithology, 159 Sapsucker Woods Road, Ithaca, NY 14850. phone 1-877-266-4928; Website: www.wbuny.com

BIRD FAMILIES OF NORTH AMERICA

Bird names are standardized in North America by the Nomenclature Committee of the American Ornithologists' Union. This is the group that determines placement of birds in families and arranges the order based on relationships. This committee is also responsible for assigning English (common) names. While some name changes are confusing (e.g., changing Baltimore Oriole to Northern Oriole and then back to Baltimore Oriole) the benefit of standard names is enormous and reduces much confusion that is common among other plant and animal groups that lack nomenclature committees. Changes are necessary because research continuously sheds new light on bird relationships.

The numbers of birds that are presently in families will change over time as bird ranges change and as our understanding of relationships changes. New species will venture into North America and world numbers may change as a few new species may be discovered. Tragically, some species will also become extinct. Most changes, however, will result in our increasing knowledge about bird relationships. Recently, some forms thought to be the same are now believed to be different, while other forms thought to be different are now believed to be the same (or hybrids.)

Bird families are not always specific enough to help identifications at the species level. For this reason, the following list presents eighty-eight families, subfamilies, and other groupings that are recognizable in the field. The family and subfamily names are from the American Ornithologists' Union's 7th edition (1998) *Check List of North American Birds*.

Gaviiformes
  Loons: Gaviidae
Podicipediformes
  Grebes: Podicipedidae
Procellariiformes
  Albatrosses: Diomedeidae
  Shearwaters and Petrels: Procellariidae
  Storm-Petrels: Hydrobatidae
Pelecaniformes
  Tropicbirds: Phaethontidae
  Boobies and Gannets: Sulidae
  Pelicans: Pelecanidae
  Cormorants: Phalacrocoracidae
  Anhingas: Anhingidae
  Frigatebirds: Fregatidae
Ciconiiformes
  Herons and Bitterns: Ardeidae
  Ibises and Spoonbills: Threskiornithidae
  Storks: Ciconiidae
  New World Vultures: Cathartidae
Anseriformes
  Ducks, Geese, and Swans: Anatidae
    Whistling-Ducks: Dendrocygninae
    Geese and Swans: Anserinae
    True Ducks: Anatinae
Falconiformes
  Osprey, Hawks, Kites, and Eagles: Accipitridae
    Ospreys: Pandioninae
    Kites, Eagles and Hawks: Accipitrinae
  Caracaras and Falcons: Falconidae
    Caracaras: Caracarinae
    Falcons: Falconinae
Galliformes
  Chachalaca: Cracidae
  Grouse, Partridges, and Turkeys: Phasianidae
    Partridges and Pheasants: Phasianinae
    Grouse: Tetraoninae
    Turkeys: Meleagridinae
  New World Quail: Odontophoridae

Gruiformes
  Rails, Gallinules, and Coots: Rallidae
  Limpkins: Aramidae
  Cranes: Gruidae
Charadriiformes
  Plovers: Chraradriidae
  Oystercatchers: Haematopodidae
  Stilts and Avocets: Recurvirostridae
  Sandpipers, Phalaropes, and allies: Scolopacidae
  Gulls, Terns, and Skimmers: Laridae
    Skuas and Jaegers: Stercorariinae
    Gulls: Larinae
    Terns: Sterninae
    Skimmers: Rynchopinae
  Auks, Murres, and Puffins: Alcidae
Columbiformes
  Pigeons and Doves: Columbidae
Psittaciformes
  Parrots and Parakeets: Psittacidae
Cuculiformes
  Cuckoos, Anis, and Roadrunners: Cuculidae
    New World Cuckoos: Coccyzinae
    Roadrunners: Neomorphinae
    Anis: Crotophaginae
Strigiformes
  Barn Owls: Tytonidae
  Typical Owls: Strigidae
Caprimulgiformes
  Goatsuckers and Nighthawks: Caprimulgidae
Apodiformes
  Swifts: Apodidae
  Hummingbirds: Trochilidae
Trogoniformes
  Trogons: Trogonidae
Coraciiformes
  Kingfishers: Alcedinidae
Piciformes
  Woodpeckers: Picidae

Passeriformes
    Tyrant Flycatchers: Tyrannidae
    Shrikes: Laniidae
    Vireos: Vireonidae
    Crows and Jays: Corvidae
    Larks: Alaudidae
    Swallows: Hirundinidae
    Chickadees and Titmice: Paridae
    Verdins: Remizidae
    Bushtits: Aegithalidae
    Nuthatches: Sittidae
    Creepers: Certhiidae
    Wrens: Troglodytidae
    Dippers: Cinclidae
    Kinglets: Regulidae
    Old World Warblers and Gnatcatchers: Sylviidae
        Old World Warblers: Sylviinae
        Gnatcatchers: Polioptilinae

    Thrushes: Turdidae
    Wrentits: Timaliidae
    Mockingbirds and Thrashers: Mimidae
    Starlings: Sturnidae
    Wagtails and Pipits: Motacillidae
    Waxwings: Bombycillidae
    Silky-flycatchers: Ptilogonatidae
    Olive Warbler: Peucedramidae
    Wood-Warblers: Parulidae
    Tanagers: Thraupidae
    New World Sparrows, Towhees, and Juncos: Emberizidae
    Cardinals: Cardinalidae
    Blackbirds: Icteridae
    Finches: Fringillidae
    Old World Sparrows: Passeridae

NATIONAL AUDUBON SOCIETY MISSION STATEMENT

The mission of National Audubon Society is to conserve and restore natural ecosystems, focusing on birds, other wildlife, and their habitats for the benefit of humanity and the earth's biological diversity.

One of the largest, most effective environmental organizations, Audubon has 550,000 members, 100 sanctuaries and nature centers, and 508 chapters in the Americas, plus a professional staff of scientists, lobbyists, lawyers, policy analysts, and educators.

The award-winning *Audubon* magazine, published six times a year and sent to all members, carries outstanding articles and color photography on wildlife and nature, presenting in-depth reports on critical environmental issues, as well as conservation news and commentary. Audubon also publishes *Audubon Adventures*, a children's newsletter reaching 450,000 students in grades 4-6. Through ecology camps and workshops in Maine, Connecticut, and Wyoming, Audubon offers professional development for educators and activists; through Audubon Expedition Institute in Belfast, Maine, the society offers unique, traveling undergraduate and graduate degree programs in environmental education.

National Audubon Society also sponsors books, field guides, and CD-ROM programs, plus nature travel to exotic places like Africa, Antarctica, Baja California, Patagonia, and the Galapagos Islands. For information about how to become an Audubon member, subscribe to *Audubon Adventures*, or learn more about the society's camps and workshops, please write or call:

National Audubon Society
Membership Dept.
700 Broadway
New York, New York 10003
800-274-4201 or 212-979-3000
http://www.audubon.org/

INDEX

PHOTOGRAPHY CREDITS

Abbreviations: b=bottom, t=top, c=center, l=left, r=right

Dorling Kindersley: ic, iv, ixbc, viii, xbc, 62, 3br, 3tr, 7tr, 14cr, 15br, 15tr, 16br, 17br, 21br, 24tr, 27tr, 34l, 36br, 40r, 43bl, 44cl, 50tr, 53, 55, 59c, 59tl, 61bl, 61br, 61tr, 64bl, 64cl, 65l, 65tr, 66l, 66tr, 70c, 71bc, 74bl, 76bc, 76l, 78, 79, 81br, 93br, 94bl, 100cl, 104cl, 107cl, 108tl, 110tl, 111bl, 112tr, 114bl, 115tl, 116cr, 117br.

AGENCIES AND PHOTOGRAPHERS:
Cliff Beittel 43c. **Steve Bentsen** 105tr. **Birds As Art:** Arthur Morris 34r, 44tr. **Bushnell:** 29, 27bl, 28cr. **Corbis:** Ron Austing-Frank Lane Picture Agency 54bl; Jonathan Blair 46tl; D. Robert Franz 80; Raymond Gehman II, 1, 14bl; Richard Hamilton Smith 18, 24br; Eric and David Hosking 97tr; Dave G. Houser 118; Peter Johnson 42cr; Joe McDonald 32, 40bl 41tr, 45cr, 106tl, 108cr; David A. Northcott 46tr; Lynda Richardson 21bl; Galen Rowell 65br; Kevin Schafer 52, 85br; Sandro Vannini 12tr. **Cornell Laboratory of Ornithology:** Robert E. Barber vi; Art Biale 3c; L. Page Brown xic, 41br, 5rc, 96br; Margaret Buckwalter 99cl; Christopher W. Clark 82r; 85l; Herbert Clarke 97br, 104br, 110cr, Christopher Crowley 91tl, 91br; Allen Cruickshank 89tr; Marchall Delano 101cl; John Dunning 113tr; Bill Duyck 96l; Karen Eastman 60tr; Lang Elliott 3rc, 80l, 81tr, 82tl, 82bl, 101tr, 103l, 111br, 3rc, 95tr; D. Robert Franz 60tl; John Gavin 42bl, 88bl, 93cl, 94r; B.B. Hall 3bl; John Heidecker 108bl, 115br; Mike Hopiak 2bl, 4tl, 9bl, 47bc, 105cr; 105l, 106tr, 107tr, 111tr; Isidor Jenkin 9bc, 38tr, 43tr, 47cr, 54tr, 59cr, 60cr, 68tr, 99tr, 102tl, 103tr, 106bl,

109tr; Rick Kline 98cr; Denny Mailory 46br; Ray Martorelli 95c, 96tl; D. S. McChesney 94cl; James McCullough 92l, 114tl; Patricia Meacham 69tr; Jack Murray 115bl; William Paff 6bl, 7bl, 45bc, 114cr, 117l; K. Parks 89br; O. S. Pettingill 39tr, 100tr, 117tr; James Sanford 112cl; Frank Schleicher 90tr, 97cl; Bob Schmitz 99br; Johann Schumacher 84t, 92tr; S. & W. Spofford 107tl; P. & S. Stettenhein xtr; W. T. Stitt 92br; Mary Tremaine; 46l; 98bl, 102bl Charles Walcott 12tr; Lawrence Wales 101br, 103br; Richard N. White 80r; Ted Wilcox 2br; J. R. Woodward ixtl, 44bl, 71tl, 71cl 71cr, 113cl, 116bl; N. Worden 77r; unknown staff member 43br. **ENP Images:** Michael Durham 35r; Steve Gettle 22br, 36br, 37tl, 45t; Gerry Ellis 10cl, 37bl, 39tl, Gregory K W. Werck 100c, 11br, 114, 15bl, 30br, 31tr, 35tl, 67br, 72l, 72tr, 72br, 73tl, 73bl, 73cr, 74r, 77tr, 77bl, 83tr, 84b, 104tr. **Anthony Mercieca** 38br. **Pentax** 26br, 28br. **Photo Researchers, Inc.:** John Bova 51tr; Tim Davis 56; Bill Dyer 13tl; Richard R. Hansen 41cl; S. Jonasson 41tl; Pat & Tom Leeson 39c; George D. Lepp 49t; Jeff Lepore 42tl, 45cl, 47tl; Anthony Mercieca 6cr, 38br, 64br; Maslowski 13tr, 75br; Larry L. Miller 39bl; A. M. Rider 40br; Gregory K. Scott 13bc; Philippa Scott, 95br; John Serrao 47cl; David Weintraub 51bl; Bill Wilson 90cl; Jim Zipp 36l, 43cr. **Marie Read** 42tr. **L.L. Rue** 69br. **Tom Vezo** 4tr, 5bc, 35bc, 35cl, 37tr, 40tr. **VIREO:** R. & N. Bowers 110bl; C.H. Breenewalt; 109r; John Cancalosi 100br; Rob Curtis 47tr; J. Heidecker 50c; A. Morris 91bl; A.& E. Morris 48br; M. Patrikeev 8l; R. L. Pitman 89bl; B. Schorre 116tl; Brian E. Small 113br; Doug Wechsler 112br; Doug Wechsler 102cr; A. Walter 109bl; B. K. Wheeler 98tl; T. Vezo 90br, 93tr.

The bird counts in the illustrations on page 57 are: (A) 50; (B) 50; (C) 95; (D) 80.